EDUCATION AND DEVELOPMENT

EDUCATION AND DEVELOPMENT

PROF. G. PANKAJAM
Former Vice Chancellor
Gandhigram

GYAN PUBLISHING HOUSE
NEW DELHI-110002

Education and Development

ISBN: 81-212-0873-4

Reprinted in 2011 in India by
Gyan Publishing House
23, Main Ansari Road, Daryaganj,
New Delhi - 110002
Phone : 23282060, 23261060
Fax : (011) 23285914
E-mail : books@gyanbooks.com
website: gyanbooks.com

Printed at: G. Print Process, Delhi

Contents

Preface

This book entitled "Education and Development" deals with primarily the system of education followed in India, its growth over a period and the issues in implementing the system. The main objective of the book is to help the readers understand historical background and development of the Educational system so that they will be able to appreciate the contributions made by India to education system and to promote it further and compare it with the rest of the world.

Few topics in the book deal with Gandhian Non-violent approach to peace making and to abate terrorism in the world.

All these issues were debated in some forums either as endowment lectures, addresses in seminars and conferences, by the author and need based. The author feels that the issues dealt in the book will be of interest to those who teach the subject Education, the student teachers as well as to the people who are concerned with educational development, issues and non-violent approach to peace making.

I will be happy to receive the comments and suggestions if any from the readers for modification and improvement of the book.

My sincere thanks to my nephew Mr. G. Nadimuthu and his wife Smt. Devaki Nadimuthu for their help in compiling this work and editing it.

I am thankful to Gyan Publishing House, New Delhi for bringing out this book in record time.

Dr. G. Pankajam

1

A Survey of Indian Education

Education in India has a long history and continuous tradition. From the poets of nature of the Vedic Age to the noted philosophers of today, there has been an unbroken line of thinkers, scholars, and teachers in India. The ancient seers in Vedic period exerted a powerful influence on the schools of thought and learning. Education was restricted to Brahmins only. Though the idea of all round development of man served as a foundation, harmony was achieved between material goals and spiritual aspirations. The young Brahmin was not only prepared for the education, he was trained for his practical duties in life as a priest and teacher but also was enabled to achieve self realisation and spiritual emancipation. Their mode of living was guided by strict disciplinary rules and regulations. In the same way Kshatryas and Vaisyas acquired competence as warriors and traders. The Aryans of the Vedic Age and the Hindus believed that there should be a feeling of detachment from fruits of his actions and will to work for the release from his worldly ties as it was said in Gita "Action alone is thy province never the fruit". A great poet Bhartri Hari asserted "devoid of education, we are merely animals". Education is to guide man from falsehood to truth, from darkness to illumination and from death to immortality.

The Indian Teacher

A teacher-the Guru in India 3000 years ago occupied a very exalted position in society. Unlike the pedagogue of the Greeks he held a position next to the Gods. In fact he was considered a mediator between man and God. Lord Krishna, Gautama the Buddha and Philosopher Sankara were great teachers. They thought that life could be transformed into divine existence through a process of Education.

Great philosopher Shankara declared at one point "Three things are difficult to attain: To be born as a human being, to desire for knowledge and to seek release and to secure the company of the wise. In one has all the three blessings and he does not: seek a worthy teacher for enlightenment, he will go to eternal damnation." The ideal of Ancient Indian Education was the inculcation of a spirit of piety and spirituality in the minds of the young. Thus the teacher was expected to be a role model for the students to follow.

The Gurukula System

Men and women who sought wisdom retired into the forest where Gurukula's schools were established mostly in their Ashrams where they lived and meditated. The pupils lived with the Guru-the Preceptor, after the Upanayana, the initiation ceremony. The students who gathered around teachers of great eminence accepted a life of hardship and celibacy. These Ashrams were communities of work, learning and dedication. The teacher-the Guru and the teacher's wife the Guru-pathni headed these large families and undertook the great task of shaping the lives of the students who lived under their custody. In turn the students held them in great reverence. Education was informal and took the form of discussions and dialogues. Women also could find admission into those Ashrams. A student could stay in the Ashram as long as he wanted depending upon his personal requirement. It was his duty to gather food, to tend the cattle, to maintain the sacrificial fire, to assist in the management of the community and look after the elementary comforts of the master. The nature of learning was mainly spiritual and philosophic. Gurukula life brought about an intimate bond between the Seer-the Guru and the seeker-the learners.

Aims

The four-fold aim of life according to Indian thinking were Dharma Artha, Kama ad Moksha-a life of virtue or righteousness, material well-being, life of love and material happiness and attainment of salvation. Education should aim at preparing the individual to meet these needs. Similarly the life of the individual was segmented into four stages: Brahmacharya, Grahastha, Vanaprastha and Sanyasa-period of learning-period of family life, period of retirement and finally the period of renunciation. The last stage was considered as fulfillment.

Curriculum

Though the curriculum was by and large spiritualistic, opportunities existed for the development of the arts, sciences and the trades. Specialisation was possible in the following areas: 1. Grammar, 2. Logic, 3. Philosophy, 4. Astrology, 5. Medicine, 6. Surgery, 7. Music, 8. Dancing, 9. Mathematics, 10. Poetry, 11. Dramatics, 12. Sculpture 13. Architecture, 14. Navigation, 15. Archery, 16. Wrestling, 17. Science of Warfare. Arts and crafts were mainly learnt by a system of apprenticeship, and invariably in the homes. Learning of these subjects varied according to the caste.

As there were no written books, the contents of the Vedas, the Upanishads, the Shastras and the Ithihasas were committed to memory and through contemplation, listening and discussion; understanding was secured. Such understanding, it was desire should result in the leading of a highly moral, integrated and humane life.

Methods

Whether it was in the Gurukulas or in the guilds, there was no intervening agency between the Guru-Preceptor and the Sishya-Disciple. The teacher remained the only and direct source of knowledge and the student must derive his wisdom only from him. There were no text books. This dependence was absolute, and provided for a personal touch, a human approach and devotional setting for instruction. According to the learning capabilities the students were grouped as (1) the Mahapranjan-very intelligent, (2) the Madhyamapranjan-moderate or average and the (3) the Alpapranjan-the sub normal with low intellectual capacity.

Students had to recite the Vedic hymns in the early morning. As teaching was direct and oral the students had to have complete concentration and learn. Special attention was paid to the correct pronunciation.

Education was free and was available as long as the pupil needed it. This reveals that the education of the Indian child never depended on the economic status and the class position in which he was born.

In the Vedic India women were able to get equal recognition as students as men. There was no discrimination. Equal opportunity was given to women. No disability was attached to a woman, seeking knowledge. Hence Mythrye could discuss with her husband Yagna Valkya, deepest philosophical problems, Gorgi forcibly debating in King Janakas assembly, Loparnudra elucidating Vedic Mantras, Anusuya and Pryamvadha received higher education in the hermitage of Kanya. Droupathy raised legal issues in the court of Dhirudharashtra dealing with rights of women as the first feminist who fought for the equal rights for women. The girls in the Vedic period received the same initiation as boys. Subsequently, due to some unknown reason, women had difficulties in pursuing their education. There was a gradual denial of education for women.

Buddhistic Period

Buddhism was popular during 600 BC. There were also great centers of learning in Ancient India during the early Hindu and Buddhistic periods. Buddha was primarily an ethical teacher and reformer. For attaining Nirvana Buddha prescribed an eight-fold path and towards this he established the Dharma and Shanga. The four truths he advocated were: 1. There is suffering; 2. there is a cause for suffering 3. there is cessation of suffering and 4. there is a way leading to the cessation of suffering, the eight fold paths are: 1. Right views, 2. Right resolved, 3. Right speech, 4. Right conduct, 5. Right livelihood, 6. Right effort, 7. Right mindfulness and 8. Right concentration.

All education was in the hands of the monks and monasteries or Vihars were established for the propagation of learning. The Buddhist and Bikshus constituted the first organised attempt to institutionalise education. The monopoly of higher learning, which had been in the hands of Brahmin teachers, was weakened by the efforts of these Buddhist monks and nuns.

Aims of Education

Though the main objective of Buddhistic education was attaining Nirvana or salvation, it also aimed at promoting the four aspects of personality of an individual-physical, mental, social and spiritual which will unfortunately lead to self realisation. The harmonious development of body, mind and spirit were the highest ideals of Buddhistic education. In short the aims could be summarized as 1. Development of personality, 2. Physical and intellectual development 3. Religious. and spiritual development 4. Character building 5. Promotion of social efficiency and happiness and 6. Presentation and spread of culture. At the primary level it aimed at etching 3 R's-Reading, Writing and Arithmatic.

Curriculum

The Buddhist curriculum consisted of five Vidhyas namely, Language and Grammar, Arts and Crafts, Medicine, Logic and Philosophy. They included the study of Ithikas, puranas, Astrology, Astronomy, Vedanta, Music. Magic, Politics, Sculptures, Mathematics, etc. In the monastic schools education was imparted through Pali-the language of the masses, in the place of Sanskrit.

The Buddhist Shanga made no castes distinction. Some of the Buddhist monasteries became great centers of learning and were transformed into great Universities. The following enjoyed a wide reputation in Asia as seats of knowledge-Nalanda. Taxila, Valabhi, Vikramshils, Odhandapuri, Mithila Nadie, Thamralipti and Kanchipura.

Teacher and Pupil

A pious and cordial relationship existed between Guru and Pupils and their responsibilities towards each other. The preceptors must give their disciples all possible intellectual and spiritual help and guidance. Pupils learnt by serving their Upadhyaya. There was mutual esteem and understanding between the teacher and the pupil. Their relations were like father and son. The teacher was regarded as the spiritual father of the students. Students lived in Monasteries or the Vihars as 'Sramanas' or monks Prabnajya or Pabbajja was the first ordination or initiation for education. This ceremony used to be conducted at the age of eight. Till the pupil completes his education he had to live in the Vihars. Upasampada was the final ordination like convocation on completion of education which used to be performed after the age of 20. On attaining this Sramana becomes a Monk or Bhikshu!s. Criminals and people with infectious diseases were not admitted in Vihars. The Buddhist convents provided an education of a very high order for women also, offering training in self-expression and for service to mankind initially. Later it was denied to them.

Buddhistic system of education also emphasized oral method of preaching, repetition, exposition, discussion and debates formed as part of their instructional procedure. They used to organise seminars and discuss the issues at length so that they could develop their reasoning power. They learnt Arts and Crafts through apprenticeship under the experts.

Muslim System

Due to a series of Muslim invasions from 1,000 A.D., Indian educational traditions suffered greatly. Muslim rule in India influenced not only the Political system; it affected the cultural life of Indians as well. They wanted to convert the Indians to their faith. Seats of learning were destroyed and the teachers had to flee for their lives. Most of the Muslim Monarchs who ruled India were committed to the advancement of the Islamic faith. Though Hindu education existed in places untouched by Muslim influence, the emperors took considerable efforts for the introduction of a new form of education. The Prophet had said, "It is better to educate one child than to give gold as charity". Mohammed's followers accepted this injunction and undertook the task of promoting Muslim education. During the reign of Akbar when Muslim invasion was consolidated, education got well organised. Mosques became centres of worship and religious instruction. They established Madrasas and Maktabs. The first colleges for higher education were founded at Agra, Fatepur, Sikri, Gujarat and at other places at the expense of the State.

Aims of Education

As the Muslim rulers wanted to convert Indians to Islam and propagate it. Their main objective of education was religious in nature. They aimed at etching principles and theory of Islam making reading Quran compulsorily by all, the followers of Islam. To bring stability to Muslim rule in India they also introduced literal education. Muslim education also emphasized both on character formation as well as achieving material wealth through education.

Curriculum

Education was organised at two levels (1) Primary education and (2) Higher Education and established Maktabs and Madrasas. Curriculum cut these stages used to be based on its aims. Education at Primary stage was given in Maktabs. They were taught the principles of Islam, through Quran along with teaching, Reading, Writing and Arithmatic. As these Maktabs attached to Mosques Moulvis used to be incharge along with some private teachers. Children used to be admitted into these Maktabs at the age of 4 years, 4 months and 4 days. At the higher level, the curriculum included Arithmetic. Geometry, Astronomy, Logic, Meta Physics, Science, Accountancy, Public Administration, Agriculture and the Religions. Akbar also attempted to bring out religious co-existence and the Hindu students were given opportunities for learning Hindu scriptures while the Muslims undertook Islamic studies. Those who studied Islamic culture and religion also studied the Islamic law. The chief achievements of Akbar's reign in education were: admission of the Hindus and Muslims into the same school; encouragement of Hindu and Muslim art and literature, translation of Hindu and Muslim classics into local languages; patronage of men of different religions and cultures and starting of a large number of educational institutions.

Method of Teaching

During Islamic period they did not follow any specific method of teaching Emphasis was on oral etching only. Intelligent students were asked to teach the peer group. They also followed analytical and inductive methods of teaching in Madrasas.

Education of Women

As Muslims stressed that women should weal 'Pardha' the girls were not encouraged to go out to schools where there were boys. For women from royal families special arrangements were made for education. Otherwise, women's education during Islamic régime was not popular.

After the death of Aurangazeb the glory of the Moghul Empire began to decline and the efforts made by emperors to start and endow educational institutions became rare. Though a few rulers were liberal and tolerant, most of them were keen in destroying ancient Indian Culture and in replacing it by Islamic religion and way of life. In the Arabic schools the course of studies had a wide range; consisting of rhetoric, logic, law, astronomy, philosophy and metaphysics.

Education during British Period

The origin of the present system of education in India can be traced to the efforts of the Christian Missionaries who came to this land accompanying the European Traders. The Missionaries believed that the natives could be exposed to the gospels of Christianity and the people be brought closer through a system of Education. They built schools and colleges at different parts of India. Parochial schools and colleges attached to churches, Orphanages Jesuit colleges and Seminaries began to appear. Such an initiative came early from the Portuguese who came to India around 1500A. D. They were followed by the British, the Dutch, the French and the Danish.

The Danish Missionaries were considered as the torchbearers of modern Indian Education. The first Teachers' Training college was opened in India by the Danish Missionary Ziegenbalg. Schwartz opened schools at Trichirappalli and Thanjavur. These were the first schools to teach English to the Indians. The East India Company thereafter established a few centers of higher learning to encourage the Hindus and Muslims to be acquainted with Western thought. The Britishers wanted petty administrative officers to help in the managing of the company's affairs by learning English. They also required assistants to serve the judges in dispensing justice. Side by side with educational activities of the East India Company the Missionaries also organised systematic educational activities.

Anglican Schools were established in Bombay and Madras and about 150 such Schools existed in this country by 1817. Occasionally, the company and the missionaries came into open conflict, about the nature of education. Rander Jackson, a member of the British Parliament went to the extent of saying, "We have lost our colonies in America by imparting our education there. We need not do so in India also". The court of Directors of the East India Company endorsing this view observed that the Hindus had as good a system of morals and of faith as others and that it would be madness to attempt conversion through education. However, the charter of 1813 permitted the Missionaries to enter India, to reside there to preach, to establish Churches and to discharge all spiritual duties. This Charter also made the education of the Indian people a definite duty of the Company. Lord Macaulay in his minute (1835) condemned the Indian dialects as totally useless and advocated the acceptance of English as the medium of instruction by saying that Indians must be-"Indian in blood and colour but English in tastes, in opinions, in morals and intellect" and "A single shelf of a good European literature was worth the whole literature of India and Arabia". He strongly advanced the cause of Western Education through the medium of English. His recommendations, which were accepted, laid the foundations of the British Educational System of India.

The Hunter Commission was appointed in 1882 to examine the educational policy of India with the following objectives: to examine Indigenous education, primary, secondary education, administration of the department of education, education of women and finance. It recommended at the primary level medium of instruction should be the mother tongue, it should be given to all without any discrimination, primary education should prepare for future life and literal grant in aid should be given to establish schools in backward and tribal areas.

To tone up the standard of education the Hunter Commission also recommended establishing Teacher Training Institutes and the Secondary Schools with grant-in-aid. At the Secondary stage English was recommended to be the medium of instruction.

The Wood's Dispatch of 1854 announced a comprehensive system of education for India. Universities were established. A department of Public Instruction was formed and through a system of grant-in-aid establishment of private schools and colleges was encouraged. It also gave due recognition to oriental languages and declared a policy of religious neutrality. Mass education was encouraged by giving scholarships. But the missions got indirect support for their proselytising activities by receiving grants for opening private schools under the auspices Church. The first Universities were established in 1850 in the cities of Madras, Bombay and Calcutta in the model of London University. Training schools were also established following the model of Training schools in England. Much emphasis was also laid on Women's education. The company was dissolved in 1858 as a direct consequence of the Indian Army Revolt and the crown took over complete responsibility of the governance of India. Thus British Imperialism got firmly entrenched in Indian soil.

Between 1882 and 1902 there was rapid growth in educational efforts. By 1902 there were 5124 High Schools and 145 colleges. Most of the new colleges were started and run by the Indian nobility. Medical, Engineering and Agricultural colleges sprang up in places like Bombay, Madras, Calcutta and Lahore. Though the progress of Women's education was slow, at the initial stages it gained sufficient momentum to demand separate Schools and Colleges for women and different curricula were developed for boys and girls. Education became more popular among women and colleges exclusively for women were also set up.

Freedom and Education for a New India

One of the indirect benefits of the Western System was the emergence of a new generation who desired freedom from the British yoke. The Indian National congress was formed immediately after the Indian Army Revolt in 1857. The leaders of the freedom movement considered that the existing system of education destroyed the culture, arts, literature and the economy of the country. In their opinion the system made the educated Indians aliens in their own land as they were cut off socially, physically and mentally from the masses. The national leaders initiated a movement of cultural renaissance through establishing a new type of Educational Institutions indigenous in nature which brought a harmony between the Western as well as the Indian approaches, In Bengal, Rajaram Mohan Roy and Rabindranath Tagore were responsible for Educational innovation. Thus came into existence Shanti Niketan as a centre of new education in the Tradition of old Gurukula. It was no surprise that Tagore was called a Gurudev. New Gurukulas and Vidyapeeths in U. P. Gujarat, Maharashtra and Andhra appeared under the emerging National Leadership.

In 1937 Mahatma Gandhi proposed a new system of Education in order to create a new social order during the struggle for independence. Earlier, as part of his non-cooperation movement, he urged the youngsters to boycott schools and colleges, which were responsible for the nation's intellectual enslavement. Gandhiji believed that true education should give the Indians freedom, dignity and economic independence. It should aid in the preservation of what was useful and valid to the culture of India. He wanted the roots of India to be firm in her own soil, but the windows of the house must be kept open to allow fresh air to blow in from outside.

In the post-war educational reconstruction the educational ideas of Gandhi found acceptance and after the attainment of independence, his system of Basic education was reorganised as National Education as his philosophy and practice of education reflected the Indian culture and were relevant to life, needs as aspirations of Indian society. Some of the basic principles underlying Basic Education are:

- Universal compulsory education for all in the age group of 7-15 for a period of eight years.
- Education should be imparted through the mother tongue of the child.
- Education should lead to the economic well being of the individual by teaching of useful productive activities.
- Education should be practical and linked with life at all stages.

In the last analysis Gandhi considered that the goal of Education should be the total development of the individual which would help him in his efforts for self-realisation including his spiritual emancipation.

Gandhiji's system of education envisaged a new Indian Society secular in nature without any caste or class distinctions. It was an egalitarian community.

To achieve these objectives he wanted education to be through practice by correlating with life so that the child could understand the realities of life.

Indian Education Commission-1964-66

After independence the Government of India formed Indian Education Commission under the Chairmanship of Dr. D. S. Kothari, to examine the entire education system in India. The education commission of 1964-66 headed by Dr. D. S. Kothari expressed the need for national system of education along with its other recommendation, to improve the educational system at various levels in the country from Primary to higher education, Teacher education, Technical education, Women's education, Examination system etc. Accordingly in 1967 the committee was set up consisting of 27 members of Parliament to work out the national policy on education which could be blended with the main programme of national development.

2

The University Education Commission-1948

(Dr. Radhakrishnan's Report)

The University Education Commission under the Chairmanship of Dr. S. Radhakrishnan was set up by Government of India in 1948 immediately after the Independence. In fact it is the first Education Commission appointed after Indian attaining the freedom. Main terms and reference of the Commission were to consider and make recommendations in regard to-1) The aims and objectives of University Education and Research in India; (2) the changes with regard to the constitution, control, functions and jurisdiction of universities and their relations with Governments, Central and Provincial; (3) the Finance; (4) the maintenance of higher standards of teaching and examinations; (5) the courses of studies; (6) the standard-criteria of admission to higher education institutions; (7) the medium of instruction; (8) the provision for advanced study in Indian culture, history, literal languages, philosophy and fine arts, (9) the need for more universal ; (10) the organisation of advanced researches in universities; (11) the religious instruction in the universities; (12) the special problems of the Banaras Hindu University, Aligargh Muslim University, the Delhi University and other institutions of an all India character; (13) the qualifications, service conditions, functions and salary of teachers and encouraging original research by teachers; and (14) the discipline of students; hostels etc. and comprehensive enquiry into all aspects of university education and advanced research in India.

The Commission visited various universities in India during 1948-49, met Ministers of Education, Vice-Chancellors, Members of the Syndicate, Public leaders, Principals, Professors and other staff. It surveyed the University education upto 1857 and from 1857 to 1948. After a detailed study and analysis the University Education Commission gave its recommendations on various aspects and issues in Higher Education in India.

Aims of University Education

The aims of education of the University Education according to the Commissions were analysed and recommended based on mainly the responsibility of Indians to protect and preserve the newly obtained Independence and the role of Universities in this process. It emphasized that democracy, justice, liberty, autonomy, equality, fraternity, preservation of Indian culture. It wanted the universities to be the organs of civilisation, provide an integrated way of life, provide wisdom and knowledge of ancient culture, create social order, with new value system and education to help individual grow in new direction for life long education character building.

Teachers

It considered teachers' role in attaining the above aims and suggested the qualifications, experiences, service conditions and their salaries to have a social status on par with other professionals. The Commission recommended 4 classes of teachers-Professors, Readers, Lecturers and

Instructors with some research fellows in the university system; promotions should be purely on the basis of merit; scale of pay; the age of retirement to be 60; and be allowed upto 64 for professors and the other service conditions including provident fund.

Standards of Teaching

The Commission recommended that the universities should maintain higher standard in teaching with appropriate methods so that it could reduce wastage and stagnation at the University level. The age at admission to the University was suggested to be 18 to 19 years when the students are matured enough to undertake serious study with a purpose. Refresher courses to the teachers were suggested so that they could update their knowledge and teach with new vigour which will help to maintain the standard.

Courses of Study

The Commission suggested that depending on the aims of a student the courses of study should be chosen such as Liberal education, Occupational education and General education. Study of anthropology, history, sociology, economics, politics and government were recommended under General education stream. Languages-Indian classical and European language-English, French or German should be taught under Federal system. Number of arts and crafts activities was suggested to be taught, even from the secondary school level, under the vocational programme. For Ph. D. the student was expected to do original research independently. They must 'not merely compilers, chroniclers or technicians but they must be scholars and scientists who possess breathe of vision, imagination and ability to assimilate and integrate facts and communicate their findings. The Commission recommended establishing Research Fellowships in the Universities both in Science and Humanities.

Post Graduate studies in Science and Arts were recommended by the University Education Commission. Natural Sciences, Marine Biological Sciences and border line sciences were suggested for higher and newer fields for research. It wanted the Post Graduate courses to train teachers for all levels of higher education, train experts for services in the non-academic fields such as industry, commerce, agriculture and public welfare and train research personnel.

Recommendations

On the basis of the detailed analysis the University Education Commission had suggested the following recommendations:

1. Primary school teachers are to be trained properly and the education at the High/Higher Secondary School also is improved as it forms the basis for teacher education.

2. Students should have been given social awareness even at the High/Higher Secondary level so that they could become committed social workers and animators of adult and non-formal education system.

3. To have standard higher education, the High/Higher Secondary Education should be improved as it is the basis.

4. As the high/higher secondary education becomes the terminal for many stage Leadership qualities and vocational education should also emphasized at that level.

5. Uniform pattern of 10+2+3 was also recommended

6. The Commission recommended modification and changes in the examination pattern at the Higher education. Students should be encouraged to be

more creative and constructive and not to reproduce what is learnt in the class rooms in the examinations.

7. Value education should be given importance at the school and college levels and all the educational institutions should begin with morning assembly with inter-religious prayer.

8. Women's education is to be given importance without any discrimination between boys and girls. Home Science could be taught to both the sexes. Pay of the women teachers should be same as that of men teachers.

9. Education should also develop and promote patriotism among the students to preserve our democracy.

3

Secondary Education Commission-1952

(A.L. Mudaliar Commission)

After independence this is the second Education Commission appointed by the Government of India under the Chairmanship of Dr. A. Lakshmanaswamy Mudaliar, Vice-Chancellor, Madras University in 1952, to examine the prevailing system of Secondary Education in the country and suggest measures for its reorganisation and improvement. Government also requested the Commission to keep in mind to consider the desirability of changing over from the prevailing system of secondary education which is unilateral and predominantly academic in nature to one which will focus at the secondary stage for different aptitudes and interests. This is the first commission which surveyed the secondary education as a whole and considered the 1. Aims, organisation and content of Secondary Education; 2. Its relationship to Primary, Basic and Higher Education; 3. The inter-relation of Secondary Schools of different types; and 4. Other allied problems.

This Commission surveyed the previous Commissions and the existing system of Secondary education before suggesting any changes.

Objectives and Aims of Secondary Education

Any education system should reflect the Political, Economic and Cultural ethos of the country. India got its independence in 1947 with the consideration for a secular democratic republic. Hence, it becomes imperative that education should promote the character and responsibility to make the people useful and democratic citizens of the country by developing patriotism.

With its rich resources, India is still a poor country. Majority of its people live in economically subhuman level. Hence the productive efficiency of the people is to be raised through vocational education to raise the national wealth and thus raise the standard of living of the people in India.

Education in a democratic country should aim at all round development of individuals including the inculcation of discipline, which involves intellectual, social and moral qualities. With intellectual integrity he should come out of falsehood, propaganda and reject dangerous appeal of fanaticism and prejudice. Every individual should develop scientific attitude and think objectively.

Organisational Pattern

The Commission recommended the following pattern of Secondary education after 4 or 5 years of Primary, or Junior Basic Education: 1. middle or Junior Secondary or Senior Basic stage covering a period of 3 years; (2) A Higher Secondary stage covering a period of 4 years. This also has taken note of constitutional provision of free and compulsory education upto 14 years of age; while fixing the pattern. This was also suggested to have one year in the pre university course of study to qualify to enter the University Degree Course or professional degree. It also recommended that there should be an opportunity to the pupils goes in for various courses according to their interest and capability by diversifying the courses of study which will have values and utility even at the secondary school level.

Study of Languages

The Commission identified 5 distinct groups of languages; (1) the mother tongue; (2) the regional language; (3) the official language of the Centre-the Federal Language; (4) the classical languages like Sanskrit, Arabic, Persian, Latin etc. and (5) English-an international language. It was suggested that mother tongue, classical languages and Hindi as optional and English be taught in Secondary Schools. At the same time wider option was also given to study any language including foreign languages.

Curriculum in Secondary Education

Instead of having a curriculum based on the admission to the colleges and examination oriented the Commission suggested that the curriculum should help the pupil's all round development according to their capacity and interest and cater to the wide range of occupations, activities and experiences. Curriculum should be based on the entire activities and experiences that go on in the school, some time even outside the school in the community; it should have flexibility to suit the individual differences requirement and abilities and the curriculum should be related to the community life and need-an organic link should be established.

Method of Teaching

For implementing the curriculum we need to have right methods of teaching and teachers. Good methods which are psychologically and socially sound will raise the quality of life. So the teachers must choose the right methods of teaching keeping in mind the end product, by promoting good habits, values, attitudes and skills, rather than mere memorising the whole textbooks as being done now. This is because the teachers follow mainly the oral method of teaching. Activity based methods, Library reading, creative writing and independent work should be encouraged. To create discipline and for good character formation which will help the individuals have concern for the community, the Commission suggested that parents, teachers, the general public should come forward by providing moral instruction and more activities to students.

Examination and Evaluation

Though the Commission recorded both internal and external examinations, it is not in favour to frequent external examinations. Internal, periodical tests and examinations should be taken into consideration for provision, instead of depending on the external annual examination only. Proper records are to be maintained on the performance of pupils in the internal tests-they are practical. This cumulative record will help to decide the performance of students even at the end examination. Teachers should be careful in assessing and maintaining the records of the performance of the pupils in the tests and examinations.

Teachers

If we want to improve the quality of education, the teachers have to play a very important role. Teachers' personal qualities. educational qualifications, professional training and the place that teachers occupy in the school and the society have to be considered. Teachers' present mood of discontent and frustration should be removed and their status and their conditions of service should be improved. At the same time the qualifications, experience and to other requirements prescribed periodically by the department of education

The secondary education as its concluding remarks it has stated "The Secondary School as we visualise". It has suggested that (1) we should provide rich, pleasant and stimulating environment which will evoke the manifold interests of pupils and make learning a joyful experience; (2) promote extra curricular activities by providing schemes of hobbies, projects and other activities; (3) make provision for craft and productive work; (4) provision of School Library Service; (5) making School as a centre of community-Community School; (6) re-orientation of teachers and (7) freedom of school or autonomy.

4

Kothari Commissions Report–1964-66 A Fore Runner of Education Policy of India

The Commission headed by Dr. Kothari, submitted its report on 29th June 1966, to Government of India with an opening remark "the destiny of India is now being shaped in her class rooms". Education decides the future of a country and determines the level of prosperity welfare and security of the people. The quality of education provided to the people is responsible for raising the standard of living. In this context the commission has given the following recommendation.

- to re-evaluate the role of education in the total programme of national development;
- to identify the changes needs in the existing system and prepare an educational programme accordingly;
- to implement this programme with determination and vigour.

The commission identified some problems of National Development as the (1) need for self sufficiency in food, (2) economic growth and full employment opportunity to earn livelihood, (3) promotion of social and national integration and (4) political development by strengthening democracy.

Keeping these in mind the Education commission suggested some crucial changes in the Indian education system to achieve the above four fold goals/functions of our education system.

The most important and urgent reform needed in education is to transform it, to endeavour our to relate it to the life, needs and aspirations of the people and there by make it a powerful instrument of social, economic and cultural transformation necessary for the realisation of the national goals of education. To achieve this purpose education system should be modified to increase productivity, achieve social and national integration, accelerate the process of modernisation and cultivate social, moral and spiritual values.

Education and Productivity

The following programmes are being suggested to relate education to productivity:

1. Science Education: Science education should become an integral part of school education and ultimately become a part of all courses at tertiary level also.

2. Work experience should be introduced as an integral part at all levels of education.

3. Every attempt should be made to orient work experience to technology and industrialisation and to the application of science to productive processes including agriculture.

4. Secondary education should be increasingly and largely vocationalised and in higher education, a greater emphasis should be placed on agricultural and technical education.

Social and National Integration

The achievement of social and national integration is another important objective of the educational system and the following steps should be taken to strengthen national consciousness and unity, among the people through education.

The common school: The common school system of public education should be adopted as a national goal and effectively implemented in a phased manner spread over 20 years.

Social and national service: Social and national service should be made obligatory for all students at all levels. These programmes should be organised concurrently with academic studies in schools and colleges:

1. At the primary stage programme of social service should be developed in all schools on the lines of those developed in Basic education.

2. At the secondary school stage social service should be made obligatory for a total period of 30 days at the lower secondary stage, and 20 days at the higher secondary stage.

3. At the under graduate level social service for 60 days should be obligatory for all students.

4. Every educational institution should try to develop a programme of social and community service of its own in which all the students would be suitably involved for periods indicated.

5. Labor and social service camps should be organised by creating a special machinery for students in each district. Participation in such camps should be obligatory for all students. For whom no programme of social service have been organised in the educational institutions they cannot get their certification.

6. It was recommended that N.C.C. should be continued on its present basis.

7. Language policy: The development of an appropriate language policy can assist in social and national integration.

8. Mother tongue has important claim as the medium of education at the school and college stages. Moreover the medium of education in school and higher education should generally be the same. The regional languages should therefore, be adopted as the medium of education in higher education also.

9. The U.G.C. and the universities should work out a programme for the adoption of these recommendations suitably for each university or a group of universities. The change over should be completed within 10 years.

10. Energetic action is needed to produce books and literature, particularly for scientific and technical courses in regional languages. This should be made a responsibility of universities assisted by U.G.C.

11. All India institutions should continue to use English as the medium of instruction for the time being. The eventual adoption of Hindi should however be considered in due course subject to certain safeguards.

12. The regional languages should also be made the languages of administration for the regions

concerned, as early as possible so that higher services are not barred to those who study through the regional languages.

13. The teaching and study of English should continue to be promoted right from the school stage.

14. It would be desirable to set up a few institutions, both at the school and university level, with some of the important world languages as medium of instruction.

15. English will serve as a link language in higher education for academic work and intellectual inter-communication. It is however equally obvious that, English cannot serve as the link-language for the majority of the people. It is only Hindi which can and should take this place in due course.

16. Promotion of national consciousness: Promoting national conscious needs should be an important objective of the school system. This should be attempted through the promotion of understanding and re-evaluation of our cultural heritage and the creation of a strong faith in the future towards which we aspire to proceed.

    The first would be promoted by well organised teaching of the languages, literatures, philosophy, religions, and history of India. In addition it would be desirable to promote stronger knowledge, understanding, and appreciation of the different parts of India by including their study in the curricula.

17. There is no contradiction between the promotion of national consciousness and the development of international understanding which education should simultaneously strive to promote.

18. The educational programme in schools and colleges should be designed to inculcate democratic values.

Education and Modernisation

In a modern society knowledge increases at a terrific pace and social change is thus very rapid. This needs a radical transformation in the educational system also. Education is no longer concerned primarily with the imparting of knowledge or the preparation of a finished product. It should play a greater role in awakening of curiosity, the development of proper interests, attitudes and values and the building up of essential skills such as capacity to think, and judge for one self. This also involves radical change in the methods of teaching and in the training of teachers.

Social Moral and Spiritual Values

The educational system should lay emphasis on development of essential social, moral and spiritual values:

(a) The central and state governments should adopt measures to introduce education in moral, social and spiritual values in all institutions under their control on the lines recommended by the university education commission and the committee on Religious and moral instruction.

(b) The privately managed institutions should also be expected to follow it.

(c) As part of education values should be made an integral part of school programme. Some periods should be set apart in the time-table for this purpose. It should be one of the important objectives of training institutions to prepare teachers for teaching.

Education about Religion

It is necessary for a multi-religious democratic state to promote a tolerance to study all religions so that its citizens can understand each other better and live together. A syllabus giving well chosen information about each of the major religions should be included as part of the course in citizenship or as part of general education to be introduced in schools and colleges up to first degree level it should highlight the fundamental similarities in the great religions of the world and the emphasis they place on the cultivation of certain broadly comparable and moral and spiritual values. It would be a great advantage to have a common course on this subject. Common text books should be prepared at the national level by the competent and suitable experts in each religions and be used throughout the country.

The Government of India in 1964 formed a very powerful international committee headed by Dr. Kothari, Chairman of the University Grants Commission. This Committee examined the entire educational system existing in India and made drastic and comprehensive recommendation for re-structuring Indian educational system. The Federal and steps are being undertaken to implement the decisions.

The government of India accordingly resolved to promote/the development of education in the country in accordance with the following principles:

1. ***Free and compulsory Education:*** All the children should be provided with free and compulsory education up to the age of 14. This programme should be developed to reduce the prevailing wastage and stagnation in schools.

2. ***Status, Emolument and Education of Teachers:*** Of all the factors which determine the quality of education and its contribution to national development the teacher is most important. His/her qualities, character, educational qualification, and professional competence must be honored by the society. Her/his service should be adequate and satisfactory.

Academic freedom should be given to the teachers so as to pursue and publish independent studies, research and to speak and write. The government should improve the economic social status and increase the salary of the teachers. The increment should be given for high degree holders. A national scale of pay should be aimed at. Each state should organise Teachers Welfare Service, Triple Benefit scheme, Pension, and Teachers fund for all the teachers. Preference should be given for scheduled tribes. Good contact between teachers training colleges and other schools, old students Association, extension service and in service training should be established for improving quality of teacher education.

3. **Language:** The central Advisory Board of Education recommended three language formula. In Hindi speaking area the three languages to be studied are Hindi (1-10), English (from 4th) a Modern Indian language (from 7th). In Non-Hindi area mother tongue (1-10), English (from 4th) Hindi (from 7th).

4. **Equalisation of Educational opportunities**

(a) In order to equalise the educational opportunities the commission given has given the following recommendation. Good educational facilities should be provided in rural and other backward areas. (b) To promote social cohesion and national integration, common school system is recommended. All special schools like public schools should be required to admit students on the basis of merit and also to provide a prescribed proportion of free studentship to prevent segregation of social classes. (c) The education of girls should receive not only on the grounds of social justice but also for social transformation. (d) Educational facilities for the physically and mentally handicapped children should be expanded.

1. **Identification of talents:** For the cultivation of excellence it is necessary that talent in diverse fields should be identified at an early age and opportunity should be given for its full development.

2. Work experience and National Service should become an integral part of education.

3. **Science Education and Research:** Modernisation and increasing productivity are two main goals of education according to the Kothari Commission. This point tells us the importance of scientific, agricultural and technical education. If the above mentioned goals are to be achieved the nation wide movement has to be started and introduce work experience in all the schools.

To deal with matters of science education the government has established the department of science and Technology in 1971 and a National committee on Science and Technology in 1973. Science and Technological education is sponsored at four stages; under various institutions of different ministries in central government like IITS.

University Education commission has reported: "to promote the interest of agriculture the present education is extremely inadequate and agricultural education should be recognised as a major educational issue." On the basis of this recommendation Agricultural Research Education is taken care by the government established ICAR (Indian council of Agricultural Research). This had been given university status in 1960. For the same purpose government has established the Department of agricultural Research and Education in 1973.

4. **Production of Books:** The quality of books should be improved by attracting the best writing talent through a liberal policy of incentives should be given to books for children and to university-level books in regional languages.

5. **Examinations:** A major goal of examination reforms should be to improve the reliability and validity of examinations and to make evaluation a continuous process aimed at helping the student to improve his/her level of achievement rather than at

'certifying' the quality of his/her performance at given moment of time.

The Education commission recommended for autonomy of universities and within the university system autonomy to the colleges so that there could be freedom to experiment with education system, curriculum, teaching strategies and procedure of evolution and examinations. Education commission, under the leadership of Dr D.S Kothari submitted a very comprehensive report covering all the aspects of education to be taken care at all levels from Pre-primary to University level. Infact, Kothari commissions report on education is said to be 'Magna Charta' of Indian education system.

5

National Education Policy on Education (1986)

After the submission of Kothari Commission report in 1968 the National Policy of Education was another landmark in the post-independent India though there were Committees such as (1) Promoting national progress; (2) A sense of common citizenship and culture, (3) To strengthen national integration, (4) Improving education at all stages, (5) Promoting Science and Technology, (6) Promoting moral values and (7) Establishing close relation between education and the life of the people.

The Essence and Role of Education as Perceived by National Policy of Education of 1986

The National Policy of Education has identified the following as the essence of education.

- Acculturating role wherein education furthers the goals of socialism, secularism and democracy.
- Promoting Self-reliance through economic progress.

National System of Education

The National system of Education implies that up to a given level, all students irrespective of caste, creed, location or sex have access to education of a comparable quality, by adopting the following procedures in the educational system.

- A common educational structure of 10+2+3 is envisaged
- National System of Education is based on a national curricular framework.
- Promoting the international cooperation and peaceful co-existence with the world is inculcated in youths.
- Understanding the diverse culture and the social system will be emphasized.
- providing facilities for inter-regional mobility for equal access to every Indian to pursue higher and technical education
- Dissemination of research findings in Science and Technology and Development
- Nation as a whole will take up the responsibility of promoting education at different levels.
- Life long education will be promoted through open and distance learning.

The above said goals of National Policy of Education 1986 were adopted in the Parliament in 1986.

In the constitutional amendment of 1976, education was included in the concurrent list i.e. education to have partnership with State. Responsibility of sharing the financial and administrative between the Union Government and the State Governments was emphasized which is a new step to improve the system of education. This also paved the way for national integration and quality in education. This was taken into consideration while formulating National Policy of Education of 1986.

Task Forces

Immediately after the adoption of National Policy of Education, the Ministry for Human Resources development constituted 23 Task Forces to hasten the implementation of the tasks. Eminent educational experts and senior representatives of the State Governments constituted the committee. Each Task Force was asked to formulate the action points, financial implications etc.

Salient Points of National Policy of Education of 1986

Equality: The National Policy of Education (NPE) of 1986 emphasized on removal of disparity in education by providing equal opportunity to all without any discrimination. This includes Education for Women's Equality, Education of Scheduled Castes, Scheduled Tribes, other educationally backward sections and areas such as Minorities, Handicapped and Adult Education, Early childhood Education, Elementary Education, Universal Enrolment, Universal Retention up to 14 years of age and Quality Education, Non-formal Education for dropouts, working children and girls, Secondary Education with an emphasis on enrolment of girls, SCs. and STs, exposing them to sciences, constitutional rights and duties, vocationalisation by introducing systematic, well planned vocational courses to create a positive attitude towards dignity of labour and work culture, Higher, Higher Secondary Education that will reflect the critical, social, economic, cultural, moral and spiritual issues facing the society by providing specialised knowledge and skills, encouraging autonomous colleges, establishing State councils for Higher Education, Researches of high quality to be undertaken in universities, Open University and Distance Learning to provide opportunity for higher education and for life long education.

De-linking Degrees from Jobs another dramatic step taken by NPE to refashion more job specific courses, which do not require a degree as basic qualification. Only those who studied and equipped for a given job will be preferred, not a graduate or postgraduate degree holder. The competence will be tested by a National level Evaluation Organisation, for the specific job.

Starting Rural University on the basis of Mahatma Gandhi's, principles of Basic Education especially in rural areas was another move, by planning at the Micro level grass root level.

Technical and Management Education both through formal and non-formal systems were encouraged so that it could be made available to women and other weaker sections of the society and will provide more employment opportunities to them. Research and Development programme to strengthen this stream of education was emphasized. At the same time, it was also made clear in NPE that all steps would be taken to maintain the standard and commercialisation of technical and professional education would be curbed.

To make this system work, it was emphasized that education should be managed in a systematic and disciplined way with utmost intellectual rigour and seriousness of purpose, at the same time promote innovations and creativity, with the emphasis on teachers. Hence the strategy suggested by NPE is:

1. a better deal to teachers with greater accountability;
2. provision of improved students' services and insistence on observance of acceptable norms of behaviour;
3. provision of better facilities to institutions; and
4. Creation of a system of performance appraisals of institutions according to standards and norms set at the National or State levels.

Another major emphasis of NPE was on reorienting the content and process of education. Without affecting the India's rich culture and history it wanted the curriculum to be revised. Deculturation, De-humanisation and alienation must be taken into consideration while new content was introduced at all levels of education system.

National Policy on Education also emphasized that "Education can and must bring about the fine synthesis between change-oriented technologies and the country's continuity of cultural tradition'.

The emphasis on value education to foster universal and eternal values to eliminate obscurantism, religious fanaticism, violence, superstition and fatalism from Indian society is another noteworthy contribution of NPE.

Improving the availability of standard books at low prices; improving library facilities nationwide; encouraging generation and use of modern media and new educational technology in the classrooms; exposing to work experience; integrating environmental education and population education into the curriculum at all levels; to teach mathematics and science to make the child think, reason, analyse and articulate logically, promote spirit of enquiry, creativity, objectivity and aesthetic sense, encourage sports, physical education and yoga to promote the integrated development of body and mind and youth to be given the opportunities in National Service Scheme (NSS), National Cadet Corps (NCC) etc.

NPE also gave importance to the evaluation process and examination reform to bring about qualitative improvements in education by ensuring validity, objectivity and reliability. It also emphasized that there should be de-emphasis on memorisation, continuous and comprehensive evaluation, semester system and use of grading system.

Teacher and Teacher Training

While talking about the status of teachers and their training the NPE has rightly pointed out that "status of the teacher reflects the socio-cultural ethos of a society and no people can rise above the level of its teachers". As the teacher has got great honour it wanted the teachers to be recruited purely on the basis of merit, objectivity and conformity with the requirements. Maintaining accountability and professional integrity is to be emphasized.

As the teacher education is a continuous process, both pre-service and in-service programmes for teachers were given due consideration. District Institutes of Education and Training (DIET) for training the elementary school teachers and personnel for adult and non-formal education and training the teachers for secondary schools, colleges of education would be upgraded and State Councils of Educational Research and Training (SCERT) at the state level and National Council of Teacher Education were recommended.

The Management of Education

The National Policy on Education insisted on an overhauling of the system of planning and the management of education depending on:

(a) Country's development and manpower requirement;

(b) Autonomy for educational institutions;

(c) Involving NGOs and Voluntary efforts and more women and,

(d) Establishing principle of accountability in relation to given objectives and norms.

National level Central Advisory Board of Education should play a vital role at the national level and proposed to create Indian Education Service as an All India Service. Similarly, State Governments establish State Advisory Boards of Education for effective functioning of Human Resource Development activities. To manage educational activities at the district level, it recommended District Boards of education, in which the local level agencies will also participate.

In order to redress grievances in implementing educational programmes at different levels of education, NPE recommended tribunals also.

Resources

It was felt that the national goals could be achieved only through adequate resources. Investment in education through donations, local communities and agencies for maintaining buildings, supplying consumables, raising fees can result in effective use of infrastructure facilities available. It was also recommended that funds could be mobilised by levying a cess or charge for using the services of educational institutions and education to be considered as a crucial area of investment for national development.

The main task suggested by NPE as conclusion and future of Indian education system was to strengthen the base of the pyramid-i.e. our elementary education system should be strengthened and we should ensure that those at the 'top of the pyramid are the best among the intellectuals in the world.

6

Research in Higher Education Institutions

Research has become an integral part of the higher education as the triangular aspects of education-Teaching, Research and Extension have equal importance in the higher education system. Research imparts dynamism to educational process and extends the frontiers of knowledge. It is a well-planned empirical analysis leading to development of theories, concepts, principles, generalisations and strategies which lead to action plans. Research invokes the cause and effect relationships, predictions and help to formulate policies and programmes.

Purpose of Research

Research invites discovery of solutions to problems. Basing on these solutions new theoretical frame works could be formulated. It provides first hand information on science and technology in progress. Researcher gets an in-depth knowledge of the subject matter. With the help of the new knowledge gained and from other sources the researcher tries to discover solutions to the issues that have not been completely resolved.

Research also makes an individual self disciplined. A researcher becomes organised and learns to put forth ones view clearly, precisely, concisely and coherently in the form of a report. It also demands for an original solution from an individual for any problem

It is not that an individual should try to prove a fact or a concept through his/her researches, rather it should create a genuine desire in an individual to know thc truth or find solution to the problem or to create new knowledge and always be searching for new.

Research makes teaching, learning process a dynamic one. It leads both the teacher and the learners to have thirst for discovery, invention, and innovation application of new concepts, skills and knowledge.

Researches of all types, basic or applied in science or humanities in the Institutes of Higher education should aim at strengthening and promoting the socio, economic, and cultural scenario of the nation and to lead the people towards a new horizon.

Research should have social, economic and cultural relevance and concern so that the results could help achieve the goal of strengthening the socio-economic and cultural scenario of the country. The results of the researches should be tested for their utility by establishing linkages with the community and industry who are the consumers, the users.

Universities and colleges should be encouraged to take up researches in collaboration with the agencies which aspire to improve their system, functioning, processing, management and output. This type of collaborative efforts on the part of the institutes of higher education will help the scholars get employed immediately on completion of their researches. The linkages with industries, communities, national laboratories, research institutes at State and National levels, development agencies, and NGO will attract the scholars to take up the researches on the basis of their requirement-thus the researches become need based. Need based researches will attract the users and they in turn will be ready to support such type of researches/projects.

The Responsibilities of the Institutes of Higher Education

Before launching any research project either for the doctoral degrees or a project the institutes should identify the needs of the community, the industries, the agencies who are the users or consumers of the results of such researches. This need assessment will help the researchers to choose functional, a right and relevant theme for their researches instead of choosing a topic just to get a degree or add to their titles. A researcher with genuine concern for social problems can contribute his/her mite to human development and welfare through researches in science and humanities.

The Universities and Colleges should form a network of institutions with similar objectives, concerns and commitment to share their research findings, including the problems and issues in which they are interested, the strategies which they adopt and the dissemination of results or findings of the researches.

Interdisciplinary and multidisciplinary researches will promote the totality and the common concern of the humanity. If the institutes of higher education could identify the common problems multi pronged attack or approach to find a suitable solution will become easy and meaningful.

If institutes of Higher Education establish the linkages with the industries and other organisations, NGO, Government departments' etc mobilisation of resources becomes easy. Funds will not be a constraint to take up researches. This tie up and linkages will also help the individual researchers to make their findings, discoveries and innovations easily saleable/marketable as they get recognition from many sources.

When the laboratory researches in the institutes of Higher Education are taken to the field, applied and got feed back they could be refined, updated and could be made relevant and need based. The objectives of the research, the approaches-strategies, tools and the methods of analysis could be modified to suit the requirement of the field, the community, and the users.

Universities and Colleges could also concentrate on Action Researches, the results of which could be of immediate application. Action researches could be completed at a shorter duration, with fewer resources and for immediate application. The findings should be made available to all those who would like to use them for furthering their services to the community.

Outreach-extension programmes of the Universities and Colleges will become more meaningful and effective when the findings of researches are fed into the field for immediate practice/implementation. This will be of a supportive programme and strengthen Research and Extension components of higher education institutions.

Researches in higher education should also promote the social accountability of the University and College teachers. They should be made to concentrate on themes that will be of use to the community which supports them. Conscious effort on improving the scenario of the community/society/ country through research and extension should give a satisfaction to the researchers and the institutions in which they are employed as both could express their accountability to the society through their research and extension.

7

Towards an Englightened and Humane Society

(Report of the Committee for Review of National Policy on Education, 1986)

In 1990 Government of India appointed a Committee under the Chairmanship of Acharya Ramamurthy to review the National Policy on Education of 1986 with the following reasons:

1. In spite of all our efforts to improve social and economic development many are deprived of education;
2. Fifty per cent of the total illiterate population of the world is in India;
3. Acceptable level of primary education is not given to a large section of people;
4. Make education as a human right to move towards a humane and enlightened society;
5. To make education as an instrument for securing equality for women, backward classes and minorities;

6. To provide employment oriented education and to exclude from it the elitist aberrations;

7. To move towards an egalitarian and secular society.

Goals of Education

This review committee recommended that we could have "the goal of education is to establish a non-violent and non-exploiting social and economic order" as suggested by Mahatma Gandhi. It also emphasized that education should be a life long process of "Learning to be by Learning To Become". It means education cannot be given within four walls of classrooms, in a fixed period; it is a continuous process to equip the students to continue to learn as well as unlearn. To specify the role of education as stated would be:

(a) Education as knowledge provider to empower;

(b) Opportunity for acquiring skills in communication compilation, social and manual skills;

(c) Nurturing the values personal, social, cultural and national and

(d) Play an interventionist and catalytic role to promote national cohesion and unity and empower students' agents of social change.

To play these roles the system of education should be a realistic one by providing experimental content, foundational experience for more liberation by humanising the person. And these will help India realise the goals of a united secular India, a modern nation, a productive people and a Humane and a Caring Society.

Education should reduce the alienation from the community by making the schools as common community schools which will be aided by the Government and the English medium aided and unaided will become neighbourhood schools. All these schools will play the interventionist and catalytic role. Future of India will be bright only when we combine the best in both science and spirituality.

Participatory education, participatory development and participatory democracy can be realised only where there is decentralisation. People's strength should be recognised and given the power not only to govern but also to participate in every aspect of life.

Equity, Social Justice and Education

The NPE review committee deals with this aspect in 5 sections-a) Education and Women's equality, (b) Education for the SCs/STs and other educational backward sections, (c) Education of the Handicapped, (d) Common School System and (e) Navodaya Vidyalaya, on the basis of a detailed analysis of the existing systems NPE's suggestions and 4 years of implementation of the various schemes offered to achieve this goal of equity, social justice and education, Ramamurthy Committee had recommended many ways to achieve this goal in a realistic way, including fund required for implementing.

There is a detailed discussion on the type, approaches and methods of various facilities of education such as Early Childhood care and Education, to make universalisation of elementary education, Adult and continuing education, Education and Right to work, Higher education, Technical and Management Education, Languages in Education, Content and Process of Education, Teachers and students including Teacher Education and their status. Decentralisation and Participative Management and Resources for Education, will be comprehensive, cost effective and useful to the community.

In every chapter this report deals with the existing system and how to bring about changes in order to realise the goals of Indian education which will ultimately lead towards an Enlightened and Humane Society. It has a strong base for total development of the students and the teachers who are the future hope of this great nation India by combining Science and Spirituality so that India will not stay behind the fast growing world of Science and Technology. This report also suggested that on the basis of the review the Government may like to bring out a revised Policy in the light of its recommendations.

8

A Paradigm Shift from Literacy to Open Distance Learning

Introduction

Education is not just possession of knowledge or simple literacy i.e.-to read and write. It is not even the mastery of the three R's namely read, write and arithmetic i.e. ability to decode the symbols, to express thoughts, which is closely associated with economic, social, political and cultural life of a community. It is a life long process towards a knowledge society that starts at birth and continues through out one's life and culminates only when one lets out his last breath. Man keeps learning in various ways. In schools and educational institutions he gets formal education where he sits with a peer group, learns a syllabus framed by experts, from a teacher who uses various methods to impart knowledge. There is informal learning that takes place at home, play ground, religious places etc. From the environment he is brought up, from the contacts he makes in his life, man learns informally the lesson in prudence, in worldly wisdom and above all the lesson of survival. Literacy should enable the capacity building of individuals for better life to transfer the whole society as knowledge society. Education empowers people leading to a democratic world.

Right Kind of Education

With knowledge explosion it has become imperative that everyone gets educated. It is the right of every child to have right kind of quality education. What is the right kind of education? It is definitely not teacher oriented but is learner centered and life oriented. The right kind of education equips a human being to meet the challenges with confidence: it inculcates values that are permanent: it gives him poise and teaches him humility tempered with knowledge and skills. Above all the right kind of education shapes and strengthens the character of a man and equips him to move towards a learning society; a Knowledge Society by increasing the capacity to learn.

Education: The Current Trends

Formal education is becoming costlier now days from Pre-school to higher education. Inaugurating the Golden Jubilee Celebrations of University Grants Commission, Prime Minister of India observed that higher education is becoming more and more expensive and it is imperative that we find alternatives to the present higher education system. During the dawn of Independence one had to pay an optional fee to get even primary education. Later on Indian constitution made a provision for children in the age up to 14 get free and compulsory education, with the objective of getting cent per cent literacy to make India a literate country. We have crossed five decades since then; yet we have not realised the objectives though there has been a remarkable progress in the literacy rate.

The literacy level in 2001 had gone up from 52.21 in 1991 to 65.3 per cent. In this 75.85 per cent constitute male population and 54.16 female. There is a corresponding decline in the number of illiterates from 91 million in1951 to 31.96

million during 1991 to 2001. While Kerala has achieved the highest literacy rate of 90.92 per cent, Bihar is the lowest with 47.53 per cent.

Literacy rate during the last decade has increased by more than 13 per cent, as per the Provisional Population and Literacy rate for 2001 census. This is a record increase in the decadal literacy rates of India, as compared to the average decadal increase of 8 per cent in the literacy rate during 1951-1991. For the first time in India, educational efforts during the last decade have overtaken the population growth. Population of the age group 7 and above, increased by 174 millions while the literate population rose by 206 millions during the period 1991-2001. Similarly, the number of illiterates, which was 332 millions in 1991(Children aged 7 and above) has declined to 300millions in 2001.

Disparity between male and female literacy rates persists since 1951 census but it has minimized during 1981-2001, from 18.3 in 1951 to 26.6 in 1981, and 24.8 in 1991 to 21.7 in 1991-2001. Reduction in the male-female disparity rate is a desideratum, in order to bring our country to the status of a developed country as desired by our President Shri. Abdul Kalam.

Rural Urban disparity is slowly decreasing and stands at 21 per cent in 2001. Interestingly, this disparity, is lesser than the male-female disparity, slightly though (21 per cent as against 21.7 per cent in 2001 census). There is a welcome consciousness among people on the need for education and the impact of knowledge explosion. Consequent development is the realisation to attain better literacy and various programmes have been chartered out, besides compulsory and free education for children. One such programme is adult and open distance education.

World Scenario

The United Nations has launched an International Literacy Decade from 2003-2012 to bring up the literacy level and reduce adult illiteracy by 2015 as being declared at the 2000 World Education Forum in Dakar. According to UNESCO's latest survey 20.3 per cent i.e. around 885 million people of the world's adult population-one in five is illiterate and two third are women.

People blessed with education have a commitment and accountability to the society. They should strive to impart knowledge and education to the lesser privileged and help them to tap their innate potentialities. Education has no boundaries; age, religion, geographical variations—nothing counts if one wants to be educated. Adult education is a programme which transcends all barriers. When it is planned properly thousands and thousands of people become genuine beneficiaries. We should make the slogan of 'each one, catch one and teach one' a reality to make India a 'Knowledge Power'.

How to do it? What is the role of Indian Adult Education Association?

(a) ***Identification of target group:*** The first step towards the achievement is locating the target groups who are in need of non-formal education but unnoticed so far. Women, tribal, rural mass, physically handicapped people, mentally disadvantaged group, and poor are tied to their homes without getting into formal education system. These are some who are in need of distance education. To locate the target group among these is a starting point.

(b) ***Need based programmes:*** The next step is to identify the specific needs of these target groups. Anything that is offered which does not satisfy their needs will tend to be rejected. Hence, only demand-driven programmes should be designed for the use of the adult learners. While devising the need based curriculum if we make it a participatory exercise the learners will be motivated to spell out their requirements more clearly and comprehensively which should consequently lead to a realistic and practical curriculum framing. Suggestions that do not come from ivory towers are easy to implement and are more satisfying.

(c) ***Teaching, Learning Strategies:*** Once material construction is over we move on to think about methods of imparting knowledge especially after building the basic skills of reading, writing and arithmetic. Is it going to be face to face interaction? This is not always possible in this vast country with a large illiterate population. Is it going to be through mail correspondence? Will it not be befitting in the modern era to introduce new technology of teaching including e-learning and e-teaching? Yet another method is on-line learning or WEB based learning. It is becoming a reality in few States like in Andhra Pradesh, where everything is becoming electronic. I would like to inform you that the Minister of State for Rural Development Mr. Subash Maraia was sharing with the press personnel the fact Tamil Nadu has achieved 100 per cent in computerisation of land records. Computers have made it possible to connect various parts of the world. 'E'-connectivity has become essential not only for education but also for development.

(d) ***Who is to teach?*** The next important step is to decide the right persons to teach the adult learners. The concept each one, catches one and teach one has become outmoded. Now each one must be trained as to whom to catch; how to catch; and what to teach. The teachers and the learners should be aware of the goals to be achieved. All the three domains of human behaviour viz cognitive, affective and psychomotor should be fully developed to make learning comprehensive, total and utilitarian.

(e) ***Evaluation:*** The Indian Adult Education Association can also help in evaluating the programme in order to assess the performance of both the learners and teachers. This would serve as a feed back mechanism to our efforts. Further, such an evaluation would bring out the quality imbedded in the Open Distance Learning Programmes. Quality of assurance in education gives quality of life to people. Quality assurance should, therefore, be the avowed objective of all our programmes, in order to make it more effective, contributive and become an essential component of our ODL programme.

(f) ***Infrastructure facilities:*** Finally, but emphatically, the infrastructure facilities and physical environment should be considered. Adequate reference materials should be made available. Good information centers with books, Videos and other learning materials will encourage the learners.

All universities offering distance education should be able to provide support services too, so that education provided to the learners is complete and the learners feel fully satisfied. Providing the services of multi media, computer centre and all other forms of communication technology would assure the learners living even in remote areas that they are cared for and their needs are catered to in getting education. Establishing a counseling centre will further reassure these learners and foster the feeling that they are not in isolation.

Besides all the above functions, there should be coordination between the Indian Adult Education Association (IAEA) and all other institutions which would be engaged in the process of imparting open distance learning. The Association should closely monitor the functioning and progress of the programme and provide guidance if needed.

(g) ***Hands on Experiences:*** Since we talk about education for life, there should be "hands-on-experience' essential for application in their real life setting. Workshop and laboratory services too have to be made available for training. Every learner should be sufficiently provided with related materials for learning. Further, the learners should have the opportunity of peer group learning. Since it may not be possible for all the learners to have the opportunity of peer group learning, teacher educators, it would be ideal to encourage the peer group learning process. All these support services will reduce drop out rates because they will have greater opportunities of better interaction and face-to-face learning.

The Contribution of Gandhigram Rural Institute

Gandhigram Rural Institute has proposed to offer open distance learning from 2003. The aim of providing Open Distance Learning is to help people get the right kind of education quality and need based at affordable cost. We will be happy to collaborate with Indian Adult Education Association to provide educational opportunities to Non-Governmental Organisations. We have initially planned to offer 10 courses during this academic year and offer 6 more in subsequent years. We have formulated strategies, objectives and identified the target groups. Offering education through Open Distance Learning is not a distant dream, but a nearer reality. It is our earnest desire that we become partner in reducing illiteracy rate and providing a need based quality education through distance education.

Gandhigram Rural Institute proposes to bridge the various disparities through ODL learning.

Conclusion

We are living in the era of globalisation where there is knowledge explosion due to the fast growth of science and technology. We should not keep aloof by taking refuge under our developing country identity. We are moving towards a developing society. As HE President of India Dr. Abdul Kalam envisions India will be a developed country by 2020.

All the available potentials have to be tapped for taking education to the learners' life long, and make our society a learned society. Let us move towards a learning society, a knowledge society. As the connotation has changed from literacy to Adult education the vision of IAEA should also lay a paradigm shift from literacy to open distance education to achieve the goal of providing quality education for all.

9

Globalising Higher Education– An Analysis

A balanced intellect presupposes a harmonious growth of body mind and soul.

–Mahatma Gandhi

Globalisation for Balanced Intellect

In the current world where globalisation is a by-word in every field 'a balanced intellect' is possible only through globalisation of higher education. Thanks to the giant strides of science and technology, the world has shrunk in size and has come to be known as a 'Global Village'. This term of appellation is not a fantasy but a fact. Gone are the times when one thought of the other countries as 'far' and 'remote'. The boundaries of the countries are steadily being marginalised and nominalised. Rapid developments in information technology have brought about drastic changes in our spatial perception. The advancement in the field of digital network, internet and satellite communication systems have promoted communication at a mind-boggling speed. The traditional concept of distance has gracefully bowed its way out to facilitate globalisation.

Economics and Education–Kindred Linkage

Marketisation, liberalisation, privatisation and globalisation have been the key words so far in economic reforms. Till recently education has not had not been realised that it has place in economic reforms. But now people have started seriously thinking of education in global context. Economists like Amartya Sen have repeatedly emphasized the kindred connection between education and economic development as education has both inherent and instrumental value in the context of development. The core of any economic reform is promotion of competitive market economy. Human capital is much more important than financial capital if one wants to make his mark in the world market. To survive and succeed in a world economy, it is imperative that India has an educational system on par with world standard. Politicians and sociologist have been predicting that India will emerge as a super power in the 21st Century. This will turn out to be an idle boasting unless and until we think of globalising our educational system.

Main Objectives of Globalisation of Education

Globalisation of higher education has four major aims/ goals. They are as follows:

1. creating favourable conditions for outwardly mobile students and teachers, who are willing to do a part of their studies or teaching in another country,

2. creating conditions that make it easier for foreign students to gain access to or participation in local study programmes,

3. adding an international dimension to the course contents and teaching practice of all programmes of education; and

4. cooperating with foreign partners in developing future curricula and educational methods.

Process and Approaches

India has already started the process of globalising education in certain areas like management, technology and a few areas of science. The process is still in its infancy and universities have to think in terms of rapid strides. A university is essentially a social system. It has to accept the new role of economic catalyst in the context of globalisation as it plays a lead role in dissemination of information and in charge of creative ideas. It will be a centre of policy formulation gearing up total economic activity and employment.

Sitting in an ivory tower anyone can speak of any kind of reform in any field. But when we come to the implementation of the programme we have to think of the practical issues that are involved. Internationalisation of higher education sounds an ideal solution to market Indian education in the world market and vice versa. But, how to do it? What is the role and approaches of Indian Universities in this process of internationalisation of education?

Implication

What will be the implications of internationalisation of education in the different spectrum of life of an individual and the nation? We have to consider the following aspects while going for globalising higher education:

1. The political, social and cultural aspects of a nation should in no way be compromised while partnership in education is promoted. As two/three countries work in collaboration with each other they get a chance to exchange knowledge of the other country's systems. Knowledge should be enriched without in any way jeopardising the national, religious, cultural security of the individual and the nation.

2. We have to seriously take into account the economic considerations. When we treat education as an industry where the product is enriched knowledge, we have to work out a method of supply/demand network for successful marketing of education. The quality of education attains paramount importance to ensure dependable markets. The teachers have to have exemplary ability to provide quality education to face the competitive world.

3. While designing the curricula one has to keep in mind quality control and quality assurance systems. The courses offered should be meticulously framed and a tool to evaluate the quality of education should be systematically prepared. The examination system to be followed should be carefully analysed and what is evolved after deliberation should be acceptable to the countries in partnership. Similarly suitable methodologies to teach the courses should be carefully deliberated upon and the teachers to be suitably trained. This means innovation in syllabus, methods and evaluation and teacher education.

Any reform–social, political, economic, educational–is challenging and not immediately acceptable as it involves changes in patterns of life. But life becomes meaningless if there is no challenge, sequential mobility and consequential development. Once the idea globalisation of education becomes acceptable and the implication cease to appear insurmountable one can think of the academic and administrative strategies. Once the activities and assignments to be carried out are decided, the approaches are determined the actual programme becomes less tantalising and more of reality.

Relevance and Importance

Education has come to serve the administrative and economic interests of the nation and becomes an essential aspect of development of national identity. Internationalisation of learning is founded on cooperation and exchange. For example, Mahatma Gandhi is taken to American Universities by our teachers and Martin Luther King is brought to our university by their teachers. Senator Fulbright speaks of educational exchange as 'from the standpoint of future world peace and order, probably the most important and potentially rewarding of our foreign policy activities'. The exchange programmes will produce thousands of young men and women "who may go back to their countries with a deeper emotional attachment to their own nation and often with a deeper nationalism than the one with which they came' as remarked by Scientist Karl Wolfgang Deutch. Besides, educational exchange establishes bonds of friendship that transcend national boundaries and lays the foundation for shared and common understanding.

Looking before Leaping

So many queries are to be answered before the final launching of this venture. Will internationalisation stabilise itself as an integral part of higher education? Will it be a solution to the problem of multicultural society? Will it bring the local and global into perfect harmony or is it a means to merge multiculturalism? Will it pave the way for world peace and mutual understanding? Is it really the process of integrating an international/intercultural dimension into the teaching, research and service function of the institution as defined by Institutional Management of Higher Education (IMHE)? Is it cost effective? Is it economically, socially, culturally viable? Answers to these are to be found only through experiments. We have to take some definite steps. As President Bush has remarked 'International exchanges are not a great tide to sweep away all difference. But they will slowly wear away obstacles to peace us surely as water weans away a hard stone'. We have to take some definite step for 'promoting vigorously the internationalisation of our institutions and the global competence and literacy of our students as being essential to the long term pursuit of a more peaceful world where international understanding and cooperation in solving problems will be increasingly critical for the quality of life and sustained economics, social and cultural development.'

Small Steps before a Giant Leap

Once we decide to accept the challenges of globalisation of higher education we have to start optimistically planning the actual process. Academic planning and administrative support are the two sides of educational system. From the academic side we have to think of globalising education in two phases–one is offering a partial programme where one or two interchangeable papers will be offered in a course by the two countries. The other option is a full course which takes care of the entire programme. The next step will be to design a suitable syllabus followed by evolving suitable methodology of teaching and subsequent evaluation strategies. The administrative side will concentrate on providing proper infrastructure, recruitment of staff, deciding the fee structure, providing accommodation and boarding facilities, publicity preparing brochure etc. The list is long and daunting. Nevertheless break ups always facilitate long term/short term planning meticulously.

Globalisation

The purpose of globalisation of Indian education according to the Ministry of Human Resource Development is threefold. Globalisation of education helps the government learn foreign exchange, quality of education is improved and it gives India an opportunity to spread its culture and values. Indian universities have a major role to play. To quote Dr. S. Radhakrishnan:

"He indeed must be blind who does not see that mighty are the political changes; far deeper are the fundamental question which will be decided by what happens in the universities".

India is a vast country with diverse culture. It may not be possible to propagate a universal model to meet all the challenges. Each university may have to develop depending upon the expertise it has and the local conditions, its own innovative strategy to meet the challenges.

10

Quality Assurance in Higher Education in the Context of Globalisation

Acharya Vinobaji, one of the great disciples of Mahatma Gandhi said "Jai Jagat" means "Hail the World". His concern for the welfare and development of the world made him feel that the whole world is a community "Vasudhaiva Kudumbakam"; it is a big, extended family and there should be universal brotherhood and world government. A global village was not thought to be an utopian ideal even in the yester years.

There is information revolution today due to inventions and discoveries in science and technology. The world is changing very fast. Change means growth and development that cannot be resisted. At the same time we have to be conscious that we don't lose our identity–the Indian culture, the ethos of Indian tradition and knowledge, as India has initiated and contributed to the world the knowledge on Philosophy, Logic, Grammar, Astronomy, Mathematics, Medicine and Languages along with the best form of governance. Though India took the lead, due to lack of infrastructure, and scientific probing we had to stay back in the 'knowledge race' and the rich countries won the race and developed in the scientific achievements. It is high time that we started our race with the developed countries and proved that India is capable of winning the race with its people from different walks of life from Farmers to Professors, Scientists, Politicians, Industrialists and Craftsmen. Every one has something to contribute to the development of this country and certainly has his/her share in enjoying the fruit of their labour and the progress of the country.

Education-An Instrument of Growth and Development

Knowledge is power. When I say knowledge I don't mean just memorising and expressing it in the examinations and getting a degree. I mean here bringing out the hidden, real potentials of the human being by promoting problem solving ability, creative thinking, discovering, the skill of unearthing the hidden treasures and the skills. Only this knowledge could create an environment to compete with the rest of the world. This type of education alone can bring change leading to growth and development. It will make an individual feel that he/she could stand on one's own legs without depending upon others or being a burden to the world. Knowledge should become the instrument for creative thinking and action. As it is said thinking should make an individual act. This action should lead to production. Intellectual knowledge, thus becomes an essential component for every one so that every one becomes a 'Think Tank' providing the benefits of thinking purposefully.

It is therefore, our prime task to bring back an action and activity oriented education system, as it was there during 2000 BC in Nalanda and Takshashila in India of which we have to be proud. How great it was to have 2000 teachers and 10000 students/scholars from different parts of the world living and getting higher education together in Nalanda. They lived in Monasteries and Chatlyas which were the place of learning. The buildings were not only comfortable for living but built with great architectural skill and designs. Astronomy and Mathematics which are the basis for all the scientific discoveries today were taught in these ancient educational institutions of higher learning.

Education–Indian Scenario

As per the Census Report of 2001 there is considerable growth, though slow, in the literacy rate in India from 14% in 1947 at the time of India's Independence to 65.38% in 2001 : male 75.85% and female 54.16%. Though there is a massive gap in the literacy rate of male and female its growth is visible. Similarly the enrolment rate in primary schools is from 50 to 90 per cent and at the higher education it is only 6% of the target population. In 1857 there were only three universities in India–Bombay, Calcutta, Madras–established by the British. At the time of Independence in 1947 there were 20 universities and 500 colleges in India. Now the number has gone upto 300 universities, 15000 colleges; 3. 51 lakh teachers working with an enrolment of about 94 lakhs which is 10% of the total enrolment of the whole world, in higher education institutions. Similarly, there are 552 technical institutions like Engineering colleges and Polytechnics with an enrolment of 2.28 lakhs of students. There are also about 185 Postgraduate research institutions producing 16800 scholars every year.

When there is so much increase in the higher education institutions and in its strength have we allotted in our budget the fund needed to improve the quality of education? Is there proportionate increase in the infrastructure like building, equipment, laboratories, libraries etc? Are we providing quality education at the higher educational institutions with adequately qualified teachers? In the Union Budget the allocation for higher education is hardly 6 per cent due to resource crisis Then how could the needed infrastructure be provided to the higher education institutions and improve the quality of education? If the Government is not in a position to earmark adequate fund for higher education, how could mass higher Education be provided effectively? Eventually, Privatisation is the next alternative which is inevitable. How could then the quality of the higher education system be ensured? What mechanism are we contemplating?

Quality in Higher Education

By quality we mean the excellence in education in terms of its values, functionality and marketability. When National Assessment and Accreditation Council (NAAC) assesses a university/college it emphasizes the following criteria to determine whether the institute maintains quality in education (1) Curricular Aspects; (2) Teaching-Learning and Evaluation, (3) Research, Consultancy and Extension, (4) Infrastructure and Learning Resources, (5) Student Support and Progression, (6) Organisation and Management and (7) Healthy Practices. The institutions prepare self study reports on the basis of these 7 criteria and a Visiting Team constituted of experts from various disciplines visit the Institute; interacts with the students of the present, past, the Management, Principal, staff and the parents; makes recommendation for the award of grade. The quality of education is being decided on the basis of the infrastructure available, the type of curriculum and evaluation procedures followed, the teachers and their qualifications, their ability to teach using different techniques, availability of instructional materials and the facilities available for their personality development. Of course the assessment takes into consideration the marketability of students also.

The quality indicators should make us understand how well an institution is performing in terms of its goals and vision; how well the goals are decided and their sustainability; whether the curriculum moves towards the achievement of these goals and the vision; how well the teachers play their role in achieving the goal; whether the institutional climate is conducive to perform well and how the inter-institutional relationship is maintained in terms of its quality education.

Keeping these quality indicators in mind the educational institutions of higher education should function to attract the people from any part of the globe, as the ancient educational institutions like Nalanda and Takshashila attracted even Buddha and other scholars from China, Japan, Korea, Tibet, Mongolia, Sri Lanka and other countries to study Philosophy, Logic, Astronomy, Mathematics etc.

Ancient Indian education system also insisted on vocational education, discipline, physical exercise and yoga for good physique and sound mind. Later, Indian leaders like Sri Aurobindo, Tagore, and Gandhiji also tried to provide education suited to India and Indian culture, which emerged as Basic education in the independent India as National System of education with some changes and modifications recommended by Dr. Zakir Husain.

Globalisation

Globalisation is the growing integration and interdependence, connection between different segments of society, lowering of barriers to communication and movement. Whether globalisation is a boon or bane depends on how one looks at these issues. Prof. Amartya Sen, the Nobel Prize winner from India said that he was not against globalisation and countries threatened were those where the human development was very low. "There are major gains to be made in globalisation. So, I am pro-globalisation" he said. But he added, 'if a country has globalisation at the highest possible speed and pays no attention to lack of social opportunity, illiteracy and lack of health care; it was creating problems for itself."

Another Nobel Laureate Joseph Stiglitz commends globalisation as "removal of barriers to free trade and closer integration of National Economies". Rengarajan (2003) broadly defines "globalisation means integration of economies and societies through cross country flow of information, ideas, technology, goods, services, capital, finance and people". These definitions indicate that globalisation would lead to a borderless world where there will be free flow and mobility of human resources, materials and knowledge. Can we resist this free flow when we have accepted and are enjoying the fruit of discoveries in Science and Technologies? What will be its implications if we don't accept? Certainly our approach to globalisation should not be only at a higher level, where the people in the higher strata of the society prosper and the people like small traders, crafts men and farmers suffer. An alternate strategy is to be worked out so that there is no imbalance in the growth and development of people in different categories–the rich and the poor. Benefits of globalisation, if any, should be enjoyed by all without foregoing the cultural, social ethos, religious and other value system of our country.

Globalisation of Education

Globalisation or internationalisation of education is not a new concept to India. Even before the developed countries of the world saw the civilisation, India had its well defined system of education at different levels–from primary to higher education. Takshashila (1500 BC) and Nalanda (5th Century AD) offered courses like Mathematics and Astronomy which are the basis for new inventions and discoveries in the civilised and scientific world. These universities attracted scholars from different parts of the world. Similarly our traders had gone to different parts of the globe and settled there without losing their identity by following the Indian culture, religion and value systems. There are evidences to show that there used to be free flow of everything but it was slow and not so fast and significant as today. Advancement in information and communication technology has brought in a significant change in the mode of travel making the world a "Global Village".

Towards Global Higher Education

Globalisation of higher education demands quality that could attract people from other countries to accept Indian higher education system. Students from India go to Canada, USA and Australia for higher education rather than our attracting students from other developed countries, though the ancient system attracted people from outside India. The youths of India want to enter the developed countries for higher education so that job is guaranteed and they can have a secure life. It is observed that every year there is a lot of brain drain from India to other countries. At the same time the number of students coming to India is reduced considerably. There are about 43000 students from India studying in USA whereas the Americans coming to India for education during 1998-1999 were not in the reciprocal proportion. We are proud that Indians shine in other countries and their performance is far superior to people from many other countries. It is the hard and sincere work compared to people from other countries that attracts the Indians to other countries. Why are we not able to attract youths and people from other parts of the world as well? Is it because of quality of education provided or non-availability of employment opportunities in India?

Steps to be taken

1. Quality assurance in higher education system whether it is supported by the government or not should be ensured.

2. Better infrastructure facilities such as good and adequate space for class rooms, laboratories, play ground, hostels etc. should be insisted upon before according permission to start the institutions of higher learning.

3. Qualified teachers alone should be appointed in colleges/universities. There should not be compromise on qualification and quality of teachers appointed.

4. When it is insisted that qualified and able persons are to be appointed their payment should also be ensured.

5. Teachers should be given whether they are temporary or permanent, the opportunity to update their knowledge by attending orientation and refresher courses, seminars, workshops etc.

6. There should be access to latest books and journals/'e' journals in the library, both to the teachers and the students.

7. Teachers should make use of latest strategies and instructional materials available to teach.
8. Students should be encouraged to have extra reading rather than depending on the lecture alone. Some credit should be given for library work.
9. All the possible measures should be taken to provide a few job-oriented courses and every student should specialise in one or two/multiple skill training.
10. Identify possible "Study Abroad" programme that will attract the foreign students. The courses which are indigenous in nature like philosophy, culture, herbal medicine, ecological and historical resources, planning and developing rural communities, micro level planning, micro credits, cooperative management etc. might attract the foreign students.
11. Extra care should be taken to provide boarding and lodging facilities along with other facilities to attract the foreign students. We still have untapped potentials in India.
12. Admission procedure for foreign students should be eased so that more students from abroad could be attracted.
13. Partnership with universities/colleges in other countries should be established so that the grades obtained in both the universities/colleges could be accepted for the award of degrees/diplomas. This will promote the exchange of students and teachers from both the countries.
14. Even if mobility is difficult due to financial constraints we could establish link through online learning and distance education mode. Care should be taken that it is reciprocal.
15. Policy of admission and innovative practices of the institutions of higher learning shall be approved

by the national accreditation body in both the countries.

16. We should promote Research and Development activities in higher education institutions so that there is linkage between the institutions and the industries/communities.

17. Degrees/Diploma awarded by any university if accredited and approved should be recognised for both higher education in another university and for employment anywhere. This will be possible only when the quality of education is ensured in the institutions of higher learning.

18. Cost of education should be affordable to all so that students from all strata of society could be attracted.

19. Philanthropists like Fulbright should come forward to institute fellowships in India also so that students from abroad need not depend on the Fellowship from their countries alone. Those who go abroad as Fellows from India and Fellows from other countries will then promote the linkage between the institutions and the countries.

20. Teachers of higher education institutions should offer themselves for accreditation by external agencies which are approved globally. This accreditation will help teacher mobility.

Conclusion

Quality Higher Education is the need of the hour, whether we accept globalisation or not. Spread of modern technology in every walk of life demands that we have to respond to this perspective. While responding to this we should be cautious that we do not lose our identity. We should not become victims of technology oriented development. We should learn to use this to strengthen our cultural value system and spread indigenous knowledge to other countries. This is possible only when we improve the quality of education in our country. Our courses of studies should be tailored in such a way that they not only strengthen our students but also attract students from other nations. Study of religions, culture, indigenous knowledge, philosophy and value system should be made attractive along with other courses of scientific knowledge as these two are inseparable.

Way back in 1908-1909, Subramania Bharathi, the great patriot of this country said–

"Kj;Jf; Fspg;gnjhU njd; flypNy

nkha;j;J tzpfh; gy ehl;bdh; te;Nj

ej;jp ekf;fpdpa nghUs; nfhzh;e;J

ek;kUs; Ntz;LtJ Nkw;fiuapNy"

"rPdk; kprpuk; atdufk;—,d;Dk;

Njrk; gyTk; Gfo; tPrpf;-fiy

Qhdk; gilj;njhopy; thzpgKk; kpf

ed;W tsh;j;j jkpo; ehL"

"gpwehl;L ey;ywpQh; rhj;jpuq;fs;

jkpo; nkhopapy;,aw;wy; Ntz;Lk;;;;;:

"kiwthf ekf;Fs;Ns goq;fijfs;

nrhy;tjpNyhh; kfpikapy;iy:

jpwkhd Gyik vdpy; ntspehl;Nlhh;

mij tzf;fk; nra;jy; Ntz;Lk;"

"nrd;wpLtPh; vl;Lj; jpf;Fk;-fiyr

nry;tq;fs; ahTk; nfhzh;e;jpq;Fr; Nrh;g;gPh;"

The above lines indicate that even during the 18th and 19th centuries we had trade with other countries and the great poet also suggests that Indians used to acknowledge the greatness of other countries while spreading their culture, literature and other value system. We should never forget that everything should be on the basis of mutual understanding and cooperation. In the era of information flow and knowledge explosion, it is inevitable that market driven knowledge alone is accepted. Educational policies of any country should be based on the global change and challenges. By being mutual no one will become the slave of the other. Globalisation need not be thought of as a threat to any country. It is knowledge sharing and technology transfer in order to bring in a healthy competitive spirit in quality, growth and development. We should therefore, believe that "not only we are going to produce experts with admirable quality, competitive and positive attitudes but good morals as well; they appreciate their own culture, values and social skills needed for the whole world."

11

Indicators of Quality Higher Education System

Introduction

A 'sound mind in a sound body' is a slogan often repeated by academicians and educationists. The major aim of education is to develop a sound mind. With visionary zeal Benjamin Disraeli remarked decades ago "upon education of the people of this country the fate of the country depends". Education is building and maintaining human capabilities and resources to respond to the social, economic and political challenges and maintain a higher quality of life. Quality education is imperative for the multidimensional growth and development of any nation. It is responsible to raise the national productivity and contribute to economic growth, thus playing a key long-term role in poverty reduction. Education not only builds human capabilities, but also sustains and channelises human resources according to the social, economical and political needs of the nation and equips a nation to meet challenges and attain a higher quality of life. Higher Quality of life and quality education are the two sides of the same coin and are complementary. But what decides quality of education and how are we going to assess the quality of education and sustain it? What are the indicators of this quality education? Who are the right persons to assess this quality? What are the methods and tools to assess this quality? In the answers to these questions lies the practical implementation of quality education.

Quality is defined as "conformance to mission specification and goal achievement within publicly accepted standards of accountability and integrity". Assessment involves methods by which evidence informs an observer about the extent to which conformance has occurred. Quality Education brings total transformation in the institutional vision, mission, curriculum transaction, teacher, student performance and their commitment to the society, the learning atmosphere, the infrastructure facilities and the governance. The most effective tool/technique of such assessment would be through ecologically valid, field based approach utilising multiple sources and a variety of instrumentation.

What are Indicators?

The working definition of the term indicator would be that "Indicators are statistics which reflect the features and performance of an institution measured or assessed. They provide answers to questions related to how well an education system is functioning within a broad standard or reference point. Indicators make a comparison over time, among jurisdiction, or against some predetermined standard or set of criteria. They provide a snapshot of current conditions by reflecting the characteristics jurisdiction relative to vision and mission and the attainment keeping in view the criteria of quality education.

Institutional Goals

Successful functioning of an institution largely depends on the vision with which it formulates its objectives and zeal with which it works towards attaining its goals. The visionary objectives, the reality of values and, the attainability of goals are the starting points. The general objectives of the institution determine the effective functioning of the institution and the efficiency of its functioning and finally the economy with which it is able to fulfill its objectives. The psychological, sociological and economical requirements of the students; the cultural heritage of the nation; and the financial commitments of the government should be kept in mind while formulating the vision of any institution. In relationship to institutional goals the performance indicators should focus on documenting effectiveness, efficiency and economy. The first of these three refers to the efficacy with which the institution is able to achieve the goals; the second refers to strategies used to achieve the goals and the third component focuses on achieving the goals with judicious use of finance.

Vision with a Mission

Mission reflects the vision and the dedication with which an institution moves towards achieving its vision. There are two ways in which the mission can be looked at : One is the direct relationship that exists where distinct enterprise of the institution is promoted; and the indirect relationship suggests the standard that is to be maintained. There is a third variable known as assured relationship which occurs when mission articulation is independent of performance indication models

Curriculum Formulation

Curriculum designing is a major task to provide quality education. While designing the curriculum the policy makers should come out of the ivory towers and take stock of the social and psychological needs and the capabilities of the students and the social relevance of the curriculum framed. Updating the curriculum at regular intervals ensures that the institute functions in cooperation with the outside world by understanding the needs of the society and not as an island in isolation. The teachers should have autonomy in decision making in consultation with the students, the consumers and the experts outside the institution as far as the prescription of the textbooks and designing of the curriculum is concerned. Coordination between materials to be taught and methods to bc followed lies in the hands of the teachers.

Teachers: Shapers of Destiny

Teachers play a pivotal role in ensuring quality education which is the aim of all standard educational institution. As the destiny of the students and subsequently the institution lies in the hands of the teachers it is imperative that the teachers work with a sense of commitment, with dedication and with responsibility. Above all, they should be qualified enough to fulfill their mission. Periodic review of teachers' performance by an accredited committee will motivate the teachers to update their knowledge and upgrade their teaching methods. Various aspcets that add to standardisation of quality teachers, such as innovative methods used by the teachers, participation in academic discourses in the form of seminars/workshops/symposium, in-service trainings through refresher courses where the teachers get opportunities for updating their knowledge and their contribution to community life through their out-reach programme and research should be continuously assessed. Such assessments act as stimulants that accelerate the intellectual potentials of the teachers.

Assessment of the quality performance of a teacher goes in stages. An honest self-assessment by the teacher intrinsically motivates him towards better performance. Similarly peer assessment and that by his immediate seniors validate the evaluation and serve as a healthy feed back and constructive criticism. Above all student evaluation of the teacher is the most vital element to promote a healthy teacher-pupil relationship.

Teacher-Pupil Relationship

The teacher is responsible for the all round development of the pupils and institutional effectiveness is interwoven with the developmental and behavioural changes of the students. Student outcome otherwise explained as the wide range of phenomena that can be influenced by the educational experience are integrated with institutional goals and teaching methodology. Hence student assessment carried out with right guidance encourages (1) contact between students and faculty; (2) development reciprocity and cooperation; (3) serves as a prompt feed back; (4) emphasizes time on task; (5) indicates expectations and (6) respects diverse latent and ways of learning. If the class room activities and student expectations are to be bridged one has to think of a suitable curriculum.

Evaluation of the Performance of the Students

The evaluation of the performance of the students serves as an important instrument to assess the relationship between inputs and outputs of the institution and of the students. It should measure whether the student could attain the ability to go and lead a life on his own, whether he has been prepared to be marketed in the world and whether he is going to be a job seeker or a job provider. The difference between the entry behaviour and the exit behaviour is the yardstick with which we measure the efficacy of the instruction imparted to the pupils by the teacher and the learning atmosphere provided. Summative and formative tests, valid and reliable tools used to test the behaviour changes of students and immediate publication of the results will ensure quality education provided by the Institution. The realisation of objectives of the institution of higher education culminates in evaluation. Successful evaluation requires continuity, feed back, implementation of the findings and follow up.

Infrastructure Facilities

Faculty improvement alone will not result in quality education. The infrastructure facilities are indicators of environmental congeniality and the learning atmosphere provided. Unless a conducive learning environment is provided, however noble the goals are, however efficient the teacher is the collective efforts of all become null and void. Since quality education depends on the congenial climate provided to the students, teachers and others in the Institution, adequate infrastructures starting with adequate building facility, airy classrooms, furniture, books and equipment are obligatory. Well equipped laboratories with modernized and adequate instruments make learning a joy and stimulating. The libraries where "the mighty minds of yore" are preserved should cater to the requirements of staff and students. A well stocked Library with latest books and periodicals, maintained and used is an important indicator of quality education. Health clubs, sports stadium are an added advantage to promote the physical fitness and total development of the students and the staff of the university system.

Inter Institutional Competition

A healthy competition between various institutions should be encouraged and assessment of the performance of each institution by a common external committee which has a scale of measurement that fosters and nourishes the need to prove the sustained efficacy of one's own institution. Survival and flourishing of the fittest become an urgent need and consequently assures quality. The assessment committee on the basis of common indicators measures the performance of the institution. A common scale has to be followed to enhance institutions' expertise in assessment. This assessment should be a continuous process to see the progress made over a period of time on the basis of previous assessment. The instrument thus prepared for the reassessments should be different from the initial assessment.

Partnership and Linkages for Development

One of the emerging concepts of quality Higher Education is that partnership with neighbouring countries and internationalisation of education will modernize education system and introduce innovative techniques to improve the quality of education in the competitive market. Without compromising one's own culture, ethics and values one can get the benefit of vicarious learning. Knowledge is one of the resources for the development of mankind. This gets created and enhanced by the interaction of human beings with nature and also among themselves. New technologies and communication system escalate the rapid growth of knowledge and knowledge gained through partnership widens the horizons of opportunities. The present crisis in higher education has thrown up many challenges that include relevance and quality of education, the gradual process of internationalisation of education so that not only students and faculty cross the borders but even the systems of education are carried across continents along with institutional and organisational structures and systems of management and funding.

Conclusion

To conclude the mission and specific goals and the functions and roles of higher education have to be linked to the needs of national development in general and the marginalised in particular. For a balanced curriculum a broad field approach should be adopted. Indicators system should serve both accountability and improvement purpose. Institutional performance assessment and benchmarks should be implemented on a realistic practical level. As the stakeholders of education the academicians and administrators are committed to ensuring quality and enhancing excellence in education. Quality Education is a reality if educational authorities are made to realise the need of the hour through suitable publications so that they could set the machinery in motion for required change. A course of training has to be evolved for the Lecturers in teacher training institutions, and training schools; for Lecturers in Arts and Science Colleges and for secondary teachers as well so that the proper perspective of quality education would be established for the teaching at all levels.

12

Quality Education–The Need of the Hour

Introduction

A 'sound mind in a sound body' is a slogan oft repeated by academicians and educationist. The main aim of education is to develop a sound mind. With visionary zeal Benjamin Disraeli remarked decades ago "upon education of the people of this country the fate of the country depends". Quality education is imperative for the multidimensional growth and development of any nation. Education not only builds human capabilities, but also sustains and chanalises human resources according to the social, economical and political needs of the nation and equips a nation to meet challenges and attain a higher quality of life. Higher Quality of life and quality education are the two sides of the same coin and are complementary. But how are we going to assess the quality of education and sustain it? What are the indicators of this quality? Who are the right persons to assess this quality? What are the methods and tools to assess this quality? In the answers to these questions lies the practical implementation of quality education.

What are Indicators?

The working definition of the term-indicator would be that indicators are statistics which can be used for comparative purposes. They provide answers to questions related to how well an education system is functioning. Indicators allow us to make a comparison over time, among jurisdiction, or against some predetermined standard or set of criteria. They provide an idea of current conditions by reflecting the characteristics and performance of educational jurisdiction relative to goals and objectives.

Realistic Goals Imperative

Every Institution has its general as well as specific goals. It is imperative that these objectives are realistic, visionary and reflective of basic values. Once such objectives are conceived and defined the next step to encourage a suitable curriculum which includes materials and methods. The materials should be need based and society and value oriented. If the psychological and sociological requirements of the prospective students are kept in mind the materials would subsequently be realistic and not hallucinatory in nature. In relationship to institutional goals the focus of performance indicators may be on documenting effectiveness, efficiency and financial commitments. The first of these three refers to the efficacy with which the institution has been able to achieve its goal; the second, refers to the impediments to and strategies used to achieve these goals; the third component focuses on achieving the goals without unnecessary wastage of money. That the institution needs to fulfill these challenges is undoubtedly accepted. The next question is how to assess the performance of the institute in relation to effectiveness, efficiency and economy.

Relationship to Mission

There are two ways in which the mission can be looked at. One is the direct relationship that exists where the distinct enterprise of the institution is promoted; and the indirect relationship suggests standards but with less precision. There is another variable known as assured relationship which occurs when mission articulation is independent of performance indication models.

Quality Assessment

Quality is defined as "conformance to mission specification and goal achievement within publicly accepted standards of accountability and integrity". Assessment involves methods by which evidence informs an observer about the extent to which conformance has occurred. The most effective tool/technique of such assessment would be through an ecologically valid, field based approach utilising multiple sources and a variety of instrumentation.

It is an undeniable truth that teachers play a pivotal role in imparting quality education and assessment should include the methods, approaches and techniques used by the teachers to achieve the educational goals of the institute. Assessment of the quality performance of a teacher goes in stages. The first and foremost is an honest self-assessment by the teacher to be followed by peer evaluation. The immediate superior of the teacher is also required to render his evaluation. But, above all student evaluation of the teacher is the most vital element. The teacher is responsible for the all round development of the student and institutional effectiveness is linked with the developmental changes of the students. Student outcomes otherwise explained as the wide range of phenomena that can be influenced by the educational experience are integrated with institutional goals and teaching methodology. Student assessment encourages (1) contacts between students and faculty; (2) develops reciprocity and cooperation; (3) serves as a prompt feed back; (4) emphasizes time on task; (5) indicates expectations and (6) respects diverse talents and ways of learning. Thus it proves to be the most powerful indicator.

An indicator system for responsible student behaviour includes expectation, mutual respect and recognition, pride, courteousness, caring and sharing mutual trust and mutual communication.

The self-assessment of the faculty is an indicator of staff credentials, educational background, experience and educational plan and philosophy. Peer evaluation serves as performance indicators that serve as quality assurance, development and accountability.

Assessment of faculty alone is not enough to measure the effectiveness and efficiency of the institution. There is need to assess the facilities available which includes the third component economics. The infrastructure facilities are indicators of environmental congeniality. Unless a learning environment is provided, however effective the goals are, however efficient the teacher is, the collective efforts of all become null and void. Quality education depends largely on the congenial climate provided to the students. Ohio's eight indicators of quality include learner achievement, programme environment, programme planning, curriculum and instruction, staff development, support services, recruitment and retention.

Another way to assure and promote quality is inter-institutional competition. A healthy competition between various institutions should be encouraged and assessment of the performance of each institution by a common committee which has a scale of assessment fosters and nourishes the need to prove the sustained efficacy of one's own institution. Survival and flourishing of the fittest become an urgent need which consequently assures quality. The assessment committee can chart common indicators to measure the performance of the institutions. Similarly a common scale can be followed to enhance institution's expertise in evaluation. Successful evaluation requires continuity; implementation of the findings; and the follow up.

Partnership and Linkages for Development

One of the emerging concepts of quality Higher Education is that partnership with neighbouring countries and globalisation/internationalisation of education will modernize education system and introduce innovative techniques. Another advantage is the worldwide recognition one gets for his efforts. Large vistas of opportunities open before him. But internationalisation has its limitations too. At no cost one should allow cultural compromise in order to get worldwide recognition. Knowledge is one of the resources for the development of humankind. This gets created by the interaction of human beings with nature and also among themselves. New technologies and communication system escalate the rapid growth of knowledge. Knowledge gained through partnership should widen the horizons of tolerance and not give room for compromise. The present crisis in higher education has thrown up many challenges that include relevance and quality of education, the gradual process of internationalisation of education so that not only students and faculty cross borders but even the system of education are carried across continents along with the institutional and organisational structures, and systems of management and funding. Along with autonomy and academic freedom there is a concomitant demand for accountability.

To conclude the mission and specific goals and the functions and roles of higher education have to be linked to the needs of national development in general and marginalised in particular. For a balanced curriculum a Broad field Approach should be adopted. Indicators system should serve both accountability and improvement purpose. Institutional performance assessment and benchmarks should be implemented on a realistic and practical level. As the stakeholders of education the academicians and administrators are committed to ensuring quality and enhancing excellence in education. Quality education is not an idle dream but a definite possibility.

13

Technology in Teaching and Learning

Educational institution cannot stand in isolation when there are constant changes in the expectation of society. Educational institutions should respond to the calls of the day and adopt them.

As all of us are aware learning is a continuous process: from birth to death. The sources of learning, methods of learning might change; but the goals of Learning never change. There were times when the teacher and taught shared the same hut and the Gurukula offered multifaceted learning. We have come a long way since then. As society changed and science and technology advanced many innovative techniques have been introduced. Employers expect their employees to be technocrats with information literacy. Computers have become common; educational television and multi-media have become a necessity; interactive Television and networking through computer-based electronic message system is a reality as a learner support system. There has been a shift from print culture to digital technology which has affected not only teaching, learning and research but our whole life. Before we explore the new technologies let us just have a brief glance through a few earlier theories.

The teaching-learning process aims at transmission of knowledge, imparting skills, and formation of attitudes and values thus bringing about behavioural changes both in the teacher and learner. Educationists have analysed the teaching-learning process in terms of the requirements of the individual and society. The behaviourist school of education has formulated the taxonomy of educational objectives based on the development of the cognitive, affective and psychomotor domains of the individual. (Bloom, 1956, Simpson, 1968 and Krathwhol 1964). According to them, the development of an individual is possible through education by realising the behavioural patterns of the three domains. Extending this analysis, Benjamin Bloom came out with the idea of Mastery Learning. If suitable classroom instructional strategies are employed individual efficiency can be maximized enough to contribute to social development. Mahatma Gandhi also envisaged the same and the goal of Basic Education is to propel the total development of an individual so as to make him a functional individual catering to the needs of the society.

Recent researches have shown that it is for a teacher to adopt different strategies of teaching in classroom to have educational excellence. This is possible by adopting the modern instructional technology. But there is no need to worry that the new technology like individual methods of instruction will replace teachers at any point in time. The teacher-pupil interaction is absolutely essential for the development of affective domain and cultivation of proper attitudes, values and behaviour pattern among the children. On the other hand, educational technology aids in improving the process of human learning as well as teaching. Education technology is primarily concerned with the techniques of teaching and learning. It is the technology that prescribes the design of instructional materials and then structures learning interactions for maximum benefit. In a country like India where more than 45 per cent people are illiterate, newer methods of teaching are essential to impart knowledge easily and rapidly. There are varieties of ways in which educational technology can provide educational services both in regular classroom instruction and distance education. This will enable a teacher to design his/her teaching more effective and motivate learning. Initially it might take lot of time and effort to use technology in teaching as well as in learning. Once there is mastery eventually it becomes an affective tool in the hands of both the teacher and the learner.

Media and Materials

Educational radio and television have experienced steady growth in this process. Computer assisted instruction is the best known interactive technology. The children of today are exposed to so many media and materials, getting learning experience from all sides. They are inquisitive and knowledgeable and try to think and learn independently. Therefore, the modern teacher has to be a guide and a facilitator in the learning process. Educational technology will probably help to maximize the educational output with minimal input. This means that mass media, radio, television, tele & video conferencing, newspapers and multimedia system as instructional aids will be increasingly used and educational technology can aid in learning and instruction in the classroom and distance education process.

Television and video programmes, slides and films can be made really effective in teaching learning process. These methods, media and material which constitute educational technology would make learning interesting and attractive. The teacher becomes a guide, facilitator, co-learner and co-investigator in this process besides playing the role of a knowledge builder. Children love to listen to radio, and audio programmes. Stories and poems having educational value through educational broadcast can reinforce the classroom teaching.

Television with vast net working could play a vital role in the process of teaching and learning. It is a strong audio-visual medium which provides variety of programmes for learning, making learning easy and interesting.

Tele-Video Conferencing

Tele and video conferencing is highly effective, especially in distance learning. Instead of either merely listening to and seeing the teacher there is room for the learner to interact. This humanizes the teaching–learning process. The tutor could check and ensure whether the learner has understood the concepts and the learner could clarify his doubts directly through video interactive system. Though expensive this mode becomes highly effective especially in distance learning.

Computer

Computer has been used as a tool in the field of education with great advantage. It is a powerful modern especially in the individualised instruction. Computer as an aid to instruction involves a set of programmed instructions in teaching-learning process to develop the skills among the learners. The computer can present drills, practice, exercise and tutorial sequence to students and even engage them in a dialogue. Computer assisted learning is based on self-learning and individualised instruction strategies. Computer managed learning can aid the teachers in the task of managing the content, pace, sequence and methods of learning. The interactive nature of computer based learning, and the ability to individualise the learning experience to the needs of the learners is remarkable. Taylor (1980) classifies the use of computers in education as a tutor, as a tutee and as a tool.

Computer as a Tutor

The computer can be used to teach the learner through tutorials, drill and practice, games, simulations or a combination of any of these strategies. This is determined by the computer software which creates a learning environment.

Computer as a Tutee

Programming the computer involves communicating with the computer in a language which both can understand. Learning to communicate with a computer may change the way conventional learning takes place. Programming requires the learner to think about the processes involved in learning. For example, a complex procedure is studied by breaking it up into a number of simple tasks.

Computer as a Tool

The computer can be used as a tool in extending our mental capabilities. Computers can never replace teachers. A teacher always plays a very important role in the teaching-learning process and computers will have to be used as teaching aids. Using quality educational software packages, good learning environment can be created in educational institutions.

Development of educationally usable software will help to make the teaching-learning process more effective and pleasant. Internets and websites can also be used for getting advanced information on any topic of study and can supplement the class room teaching. Different models of teaching based on theories of teaching have been evolved. Bruce Joyce and Martha Weils explain the model of teaching as a plan that can be used to shape a curriculum or course, to select instructional materials and to guide teachers' action. A model can be considered as 'blue print for teaching' and a teacher can use social interaction models, personal models, behaviour modification models, and information processing models depending on the nature and goals of instruction.

Subject matter knowledge alone is not adequate to a teacher to be effective in her classroom. There is greater urgency to improve classroom teaching as well as distance education mode. Effective classroom practices and the preparation for individualised learning are the need of the time. Skilful use of technology in education will motivate the learner and better achievement could be ensured. Technology can be immensely fruitful to mankind but at the same time, we have to be aware of the fact that it has its own limitations. Technology at times aggravates social disparity; the line between the rural and urban becomes more marked as the urban has greater access to the advantage of technology. The rewards of technology need to be exploited effectively for betterment of education system and for the promotion of egalitarian values. I would like to conclude with an appeal that let the fruits of technology be taken to village schools, let us help the villages to grow and develop through educational technologies simultaneously as the people in urban areas. By embracing the new technology we can fulfill our professional aspirations. Education is the foundation and root cause of man's development. Technology can help distribute education from world's best sources to all the people-rural, urban, men, and women, young, old and bring equity by providing quality education for all.

14

Classroom without Boundaries Virtual Classroom

Education should enable a person to express himself totally, spiritually, artistically and usefully . . . .

Complete education will strengthen the body, culture the mind, sharpen the intellect and integrate the child with his / her Community, Nation and Environment.

True education is the manifestation of the perfection already in man. It is education, which liberates the individual not only from fear, greed, lust, jealousy, violence and the life, thereby making the educated better human beings. The critical importance of education as a catalyst of social change can hardly be over emphasized. The awesome challenge and promise of shaping future citizen is as inspiring as it is formidable. It cannot be left to chance. Education is a companion, which no misfortune can depress, no crime destroy, no enemy alienate, no despotism enslave. At home a friend, abroad an introduction, in solitude a solace, in society an ornament. We should move towards that, complete education system, which cannot take place within the four walls of a classroom alone. It should go beyond the classroom—to the community, the nature around and the whole world.

Strategies of Education

It is predicted that India will overtake China's population by 2050. India's population will swell to 1592 billion, while China's will be contained at 1392 billion. These two countries account for about 50 per cent of the world's total population. Global life expectancy at birth, have risen from 46 years in 1950–1955 to 65 years, in 2000–2005 it is expected to keep on rising to reach 75 years in 2045–2050. This increasing trend in population growth indicates that we have to educate more number of people in future.

Providing education to all at an affordable cost is going to be a challenge. It needs lot of planning; the infrastructure, buildings laboratories, libraries equipment and teacher. Formal mode of teaching learning process involves the live interaction (or) face-to-face talk between teacher and taught within four walls, in the classroom. Now there is a shift from teaching through personal examples like in Gurukulas, street corner meetings, chalk and talk methods inside the four walls to electronic media and distance education due to innovations in science and technology. Formal education given in structured four-walled classrooms has been replaced by open learning, through on-line and self-learning beyond the classroom i.e. classroom teaching is replaced by virtual classroom by using satellite and wireless technology. Learning beyond the classroom is referred as borderless class-distance learning and life long learning where the learner could continue to learn and acquire knowledge according to his / her own choice, desire, ability, pace and enhance the learning experience throughout life. This paradigm shift from conventional classroom to virtual classroom has brought in a revolution in teaching and learning process–an inevitable change in the whole world.

Information and Communication Technology (ICT) plays a vital role in teaching and learning in the digital age. It is a boon to a learner and an aid to the teacher. Today, distance education system has become the viable mode of learning for many in the world. Introduction of ICT has made education 'Learner Centered', as it enables the learner to have flexibility in learning, and encourages life long continuous learning. Technology Enabled Education (TEE) mode has raised the literacy level of the people in the globe. Access to education is made easy through ICT and TEE by breaking the barriers like haves and have nots, intelligent and dull headed, far and near, difficult and easy and brought education to home-to the individuals at their door steps. Open learning has become an alternative to traditional learning, with lot of advantages at the same time with limitations in learning and teaching, making teaching a challenging task.

Creating a Borderless Virtual Classroom

With the ever-increasing popularity and accessibility of the ICT now, it is quite natural that the educational community should want to make use of this tremendous resource for effective teaching and learning. Through mobile computing, teaching could be taken anywhere, to anybody at any time. On the Internet, we can see a growing number of new information where content is delivered substantially, adequate contact between students and their teachers-and among students themselves-the peer group takes place in cyberspace. More people enjoy the enhanced learning opportunities and facilities. Like a traditional class held in a physical classroom, the success of online course relies heavily on the quality of interaction between students and their teacher-and among students themselves. In an online course, e-mail provides a quick, easy and reliable means of communication, and plays a vital role by bridging the distance between teachers and students, and peer group. This interactive mode of teaching and learning is an effective strategy that could be promoted in an environment without walls.

What is a Virtual Classroom?

It's an electronic meeting place for teachers and students where they can share their knowledge and clarify their doubts interacting through electronic media. The meetings can be of social contact, tutorial, or collaborative projects or more like simulation games. The communication can be synchronous or asynchronous. Virtual classroom is a place where on-line distributed learning is facilitated, a place for discussions, test their knowledge, access the required texts and other readings, handover their assignments, ask questions, establish links to libraries, databases, the Internet, teachers, e-moderators, tutors and others.

A virtual classroom is based on a Learning Management System-LMS. There are no firm rules on how a virtual classroom should be designed. Depending upon user's need, available technology and the tutor, technical knowledge and the skill needed virtual classrooms could be created. Students can download software to use in their learning activities, can learn to navigate, to find and select information on publishing place for student's work, like postal 'service' where e-mail messages can be read and sent or linked to prior messages on a topic. Through these virtual classrooms students can learn skills associated with Internet, including browsing, searching and downloading.

Unique Features of the Virtual Classroom

When there is a demand for quality higher education for masses, more number of students can learn from a single professor who is very efficient, and talented through virtual classroom. Students can learn from the best instructor and experts, thus maintain the quality of education wherever they may reside. The delivery costs of online learning are 80% less than a conventional method.

Students from any part of the globe can learn through a virtual classroom, which is highly accessible and cost effective according to their needs. Moreover, it is very convenient for students and faculty to learn alike. As it is very flexible, students can learn in the teaching format that best suits them, according to their interest, convenience and capability.

Every aspect of a virtual classroom can be automated, systematized and made electronic, offering instant service to students any hour of the day or night on any topic, according to the requirements of students.

The Traditional Classroom and the Virtual Classroom

In a traditional or physical classroom standard set of audio visual equipment, tools, chalk and boards are available. In a virtual classroom besides textbooks, chalkboard, video and cassette recorder other instructional strategies such as sound system and video are available. Teleconferencing for interaction to a large number of people from a talented teacher is made possible through virtual classroom. Sitting in any part of the world learning could take place all the 24 hours.

Porter (1997, p. 24) noted that: "A virtual classroom should not be much different from a real classroom or training room". Porter further argued that embodiment, voice, glances; the actual physical meeting is outstanding when it comes to a teaching situation. Basically a virtual classroom is a "virtual place to meet". It connects teachers and students, where as in a virtual class it is not-a face-to-face gathering in one physical place: does not take place; this is one of the limitations of the virtual classroom while compared to traditional classroom, which is shown in the diagrams. This limitation could be rectified by introducing more and frequent interactions between teachers and students through electronic media, which may not happen in a physical classroom where chalk and talk method alone is practiced.

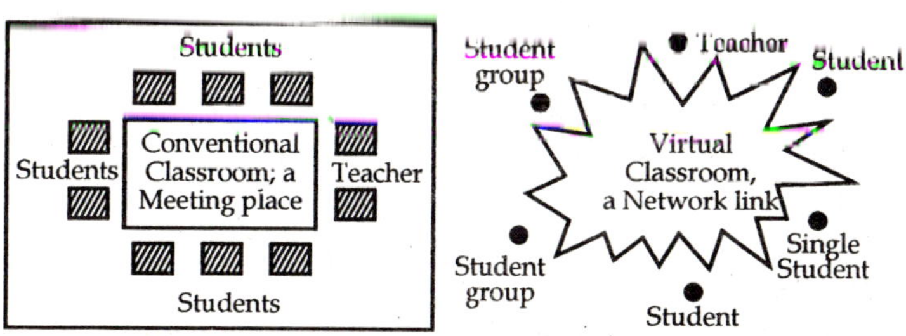

(The traditional and Virtual classroom– Tiffin and Rajasingham)

Conclusion

We are living in a global village to day where people could have easy access to each other through ICT. Inter connected global educational institutions are becoming common, enabling large number of people to continue their education through out their life. In a fast changing world with growing information system and new knowledge it has become a challenge to the teaching community. This situation has created the necessity to go in for virtual learning to update our knowledge. It is useful not only for distance education programme for beginners, even the advanced learners and research scholars are benefited through online learning and Internet by receiving latest information. Without much mobility and expenditure the scholars could have access to new knowledge, which was not even dreamt of three decades back.

Borderless classroom enables students to interact with course content, the instructor and their peers according to their convenience. Students are given the opportunity to negotiate the meaning of course content through these interactions-creating the potential for a deeper and long-lasting learning. It does not mean that teachers can be fully replaced but large number of students can gain much from learned professors through virtual classroom learning and interactive mode. Talented and competent teachers will be recognised and have more opportunities to participate in this process of teaching. Virtual learning and teaching, though has become a challenge to the teaching community, it should also be thought of as a challenge to attract competent professionals to teaching-to-teaching profession.

Learning is an active process of constructing rather than acquiring mere knowledge. Individuals can learn through interaction with their environment both physical and natural– a classroom that has no boundaries. Virtual classroom provides opportunity to gain knowledge through various social interactions with large number of people and educators and integration of on-line communication tools, could be sustained through effective facilitation by the instructor. Here the instructor becomes a facilitator not a tutor. Without much movement, with much flexibility students could receive quality education from the best teacher at an affordable cost, through virtual learning mode. At the same time the knowledge providers–the teachers in the virtual classroom become more effective communicators, facilitators and interact with individual learners keeping in view their individual differences. Both teachers and learners in a virtual classroom become active participants in teaching and learning process, thus make education beyond chalk and talk and attract the talented and competent people to the teaching profession.

15

Role of Higher Education in Value Creation

Value is distinctive of an individual or group of desirable characteristics which influence the personality and behaviour of an individual or group. It is the belief of a specific mode of conduct, personally and socially desirable or preferable. The cultural patterns of a social system are responsible for the development of value system of an individual as well as a group. Socialisation helps an individual to learn and acquire the desirable social skills, roles, norms, values and personality. Value development is vital to any society as it serves as the base for judgment reference, choice and action. Values are acquired and imbibed through a series of experiments and are absorbed by unconscious emulation of ideas and ideals of the peer group, the family, the schools, colleges, universities and the society.

Values enable human beings to live a better life. The traits which make human being move with each other and live harmoniously in a society are considered as the values or the guiding principles of life. Values determine one's personality, decision, perception, kinds of relationship and all other human activities. In a way values are like a gene which decides the character and personality of human beings which ultimately influence the nature of society and natural environment. When the genes are altered or mutated, they affect the body as well as the future generation. Likewise, value mutation and alteration will bring greater changes (both positive and negative) in an individual and society. The present humanity is struggling hard to reach its ultimate destiny owing to the stiff struggle between the individual and social values. Values as guiding factors of social life and thcy cannot be imposed or thrust upon others. So values have to be carefully cultivated and nourished in everyone and youth in particular when they pursue their academic programme in schools and other institutions of higher education.

There has been a rapid erosion of social, ethical and moral values in our society forgetting cultural ethos and heritage of the past. We fought for our independence using Truth and Non-violence as our weapons. We had a noble goal and followed noble means to reach that goal. India feels proud of being the biggest democratic country in the world because of its values and culture.

Classification of Values

Values could be classified or grouped as Spiritual, Religious, Personal, and Social, Socio economic, Environmental and Economic values. These values could be further specifically called Truth, Beauty, Goodness, Non-violence, Peace, Simplicity, Perseverance, Gratitude, Hospitality, Self-confidence, Self-reliance, Risk-taking, Faith, Loyalty, Team spirit, Helping tendency, Love of animals, birds and plants, Friendship, Harmony, Sociability, Secularism, Non-stealing, Honesty, Integrity, Equality, Courage, Obedience, Freedom, Justice, Order, Patience, Compassion, Security, Trust, Success, Power, Respect, Tolerance, Patriotism, Socialism, Nationalism, Democracy, Cleanliness and Dignity of Labour.

Value Promoting Agencies

Primary groups like family, educational institutions, peer group, mass media, the influential people and religion play vital role in inculcating value system of an individual and group.

The family wields profound influence on the growth of attitudes and interests of an individual and the whole life of the community in innumerable ways. Religion is a powerful factor in inculcating and strengthening values, especially in India. Religious affiliations being sensitive could create social imbalance also. If broad universal aspects and common ideals of all religions are not properly and intensively explained to the youths it may lead to fundamentalism and narrow loyalties. Creating tolerance and respect for all religions will promote religious harmony.

Role of Educational Institutions in Value Creation

Education inherits preserves, enriches and transmits values to posterity. In the past, India had the highest ideals of education which played the role of liberating the mind and spirit resulting in a deep commitment to peaceful living of individuals. The values and experiences of generations are transmitted through education. Values like honesty, integrity, discipline, desire for knowledge, tolerance, social justice etc. are inculcated through constant interaction with others. Values are guarded and enriched by many factors. They are especially upheld by religion, educational institutions and home.

Bertrand Russell is of the opinion that education should foster values such as vitality, courage, sensitivity and intelligence. Tolstoy emphasizes that selfless service and commitment are essential for social life. "Education without character, Science without humanity and Commerce without morality are useless and dangerous" says Mahatma Gandhi.

Nowadays the focus of education has been towards the economic and scientific development leading to emphasis on material development. Invasion of electronic media has further necessitated the need for inculcating, preserving and disseminating our cultural values among the students and help them adopt a holistic approach to education in terms of content at all levels of education and help students imbibe the values. An integration of these two i.e. the inclusion of the cultural value system and the scientific, economic development in education would promote and change the life style of student community. Education cannot be divorced and isolated from life and society.

Need for Value Education

In a culturally plural society like India we need to develop a common and universal value system through education, so that the students develop love for their country, its rich diversity in culture and geographical environment and protect them to be handed over to the next generation. National policy on Education of 1986, therefore, stresses the need for readjustment in the curriculum in order to make education a forceful instrument to cultivate the values. Development of values are influenced by a complex network of a number of factors such as the social environment, the family, peer group, the community, the mass media and the other systems like the school, the teacher, the curriculum and its objectives.

Value education involves developing sensitivity to values, ability to choose the right values in accordance with one's conception of the highest ideals of life, internalising them, realising them in one's life and living in accordance with them. It is therefore, a life long process. Eventually, the whole community should commit itself to inculcate the value system in the young minds by providing a conducive, ideal atmosphere and role models.

The Committee on Religious and Moral Instruction headed by Sri Prakasam recommended that the teaching of moral and spiritual values is desirable and provisions must be made for teaching values in educational institutions.

Kothari Commission recommended that education system should emphasize the development of fundamental, social, moral and spiritual values. It also says that "the supreme end of the educative process should be the training of the character and personality of students in such a way that they will be able to realise their full potentialities and contribute to the well being of the community".

Objectives of Value Education

The inclusion of value education in the institutes of higher education helps students to imbibe moral values and good manners. It refers to the conduct of man towards man in various situations in which human beings come together.

Value education removes dishonesty and insincerity from students and helps them enrich the spiritual values and build good character and conduct.

Value education helps students to imbibe the best cherished behaviour pattern as individuals, as citizens and as members of the community. It helps the individual to have fulfillment in one's life and also acts as beacon light for him to move in the right direction to bring peace, progress and welfare of both the individual and the society. Value education imparts the essentials of cultural heritage and helps them develop the desire to protect it.

Strategies of Value Inculcation in Higher Education Institutions

Religious pluralism in the country and in the educational institutions demands a balanced programme in value education, though value education is not religious education-Education should become a spiritual journey. It should be able to directly or indirectly answer the questions and doubts the students may have one these crucial issues. Value Education should help students develop the capacity to understand the relationship between individual and his/her relationship with others and society.

In Universities and Colleges, value education could be directly taught as a separate subject of study or integrated with other subjects in the curriculum. Value education should be oriented towards imbibing rather than learning a few more concepts and facts for examinations. Concentration of education should be on extra and co-curricular activities where students participate actively and freely in learning situations.

Activities like community gardening, cleaning, interaction with community, caring the nature around and nature would promote dignity of labour, love for the environment and to preserve it. Eco friendly activities will also help students imbibe peace in them. Sensitivity to clean atmosphere promotes good and clear health habits and a sense of beauty. Regular visits to the nearby villages and camping will promote these values among the students.

To impart the essentials of cultural heritage, cthos, peace and tolerance, we could take the students to the places of cultural importance like historical monuments, places of worship and cultural and other religious centers, and celebrate the festivals of all religious and national importance. Organising inter religious prayers in colleges and universities as well as in the villages around the institutions will promote religious tolerance.

To promote aesthetic sense, Truth, Beauty and Goodness students could be sensitized to the need for a clean environment by keeping their campus, classrooms, their living rooms clean; by learning music, folk songs, stories and dances of various communities and countries. Painting, drawing, clay work and other art activities could also become integral part of the regular programmes of higher education.

By visiting and helping patients in the hospitals and old age homes students could imbibe the love for those who suffer and learn to help, and respect the elders, poor and underprivileged.

Dr. Radhakrishnan says, "A teacher must be a committed man, committed to faith in the future of man, in the future of the humanity, in the future of the country and the world. What we really need is not imparting of instruction it is transmitting of vitality, the civilisation of human heart".

The teaching community today faces a challenging task of imparting values to the students as the community expects not only knowledge and facts to be taught but the ethical and moral values to be imparted to their children. Parents expect education to develop intellectual, aesthetic, moral, religious, social and physical values through various activities in educational institutions such as curricular, extra and co-curricular. Teachers are the key persons in this task.

When teachers are firm, friendly and fair the students develop a sense of purpose and direction which consequently provides a basis for unified and collective action. It will also enable them to make choices which would help their personal growth and enrich the common good.

The increased comforts due to inventions in Science and Technology will lead to plenty of leisure time. Changes in family structure and relationships are going to be inevitable in future and we are going to have more number of old people to be taken care of. Unless there is a desperate plan and action to preserve the values that we cherish now, human relations will get eroded in the fast changing world. It is only through value education we could shape the young generation which is in the hands of the teachers in the institutions of higher education.

16

Teacher Education in India

"The main objective of teaching is not to explain the meaning but to knock at the door of the mind"

—***Tagore***

Success of any education system depends on the qualities and abilities of the teachers. The teacher is vital-nay the most vital instrument in the process of education. The teacher is the pivot on which any educational system revolves. This has been rightly pointed in the policy perspective of the Educational Policy of 1985 as "Teacher performance is the most crucial input in the field of education. Whatever policies may be laid down, in the ultimate analysis they have to be interpreted and implemented by teaches as much through their personal example as through teaching-learning process." As the teacher has a vital role to play in nation building and in social change she has the responsibility to guide and inspire her students and inculcate value system and make the classroom a pleasant place for learning by establishing a good and conducive atmosphere.

It is agreed that a good teacher is well prepared, well organised, interested in the subjects and the learners, helpful, creative, clear, communicative, enthusiastic, systematic, scientific in temperament and committed to the society as a social engineer and builds the future of the nation. Teachers are not mere communicators of facts and principles or disseminators of knowledge but should function as the face setters and facilitators of learning.

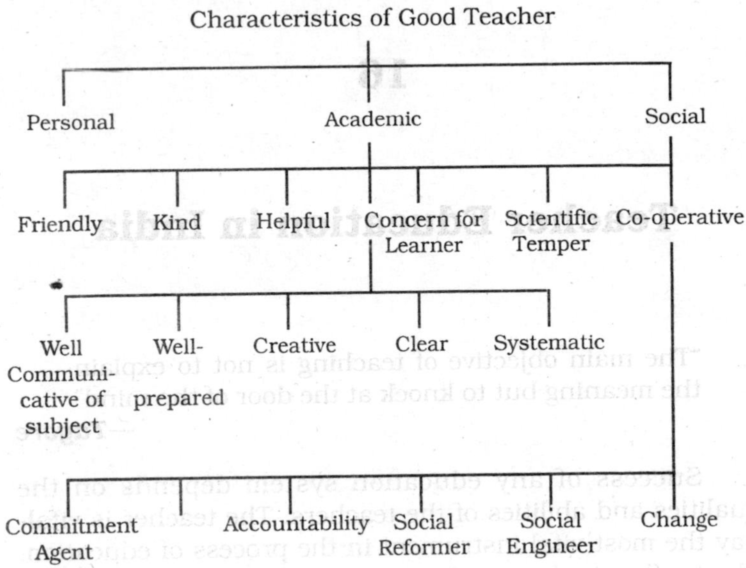

Fig. 1.

Teaching and learning are inter-related. An effective teaching results in effective learning. If no learning occurs, it means no teaching has gone on; teaching should cause learning. A teacher might use different methods, style and tempo depending on the learner's capabilities, the subjects and the objectives of the course as the main components.

In the process of teaching a teacher should keep in mind the following; Entry Behaviour (EB) of her students, the Instructional Objectives (I.O.), Instructional Materials (IM), Instructional Procedure (I.P.), Learning Outcome (L.O.) and Evaluation Procedure (E.P).

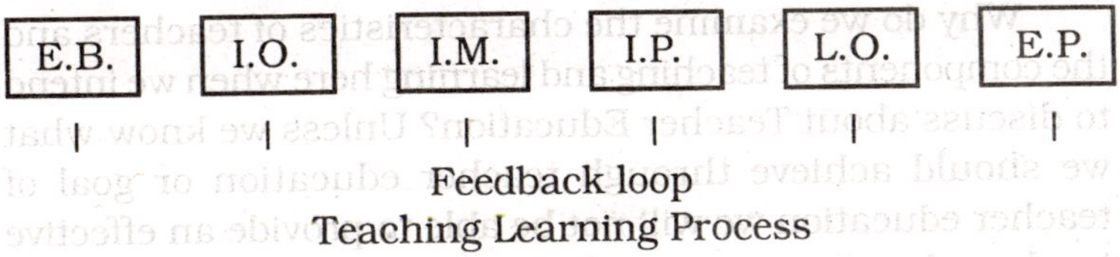

Fig. 2.

A successful teacher knows how to make her students achieve the specified goal. This implies that she should know her students, (E.B) Instructional Objective (I.O.), Instructional Materials (IM), Instructional Procedures (I.P.), Learning Outcome (LO) and techniques of evaluation. The result is the feed back to her to modify her I.O., I.M., I.P., L.O. and E.P. which means a teacher can never remain static. She should be dynamic, constantly learning to equip herself with new knowledge. As Tagore says, "A lamp can never light another lamp unless it continues to burn its own flame".

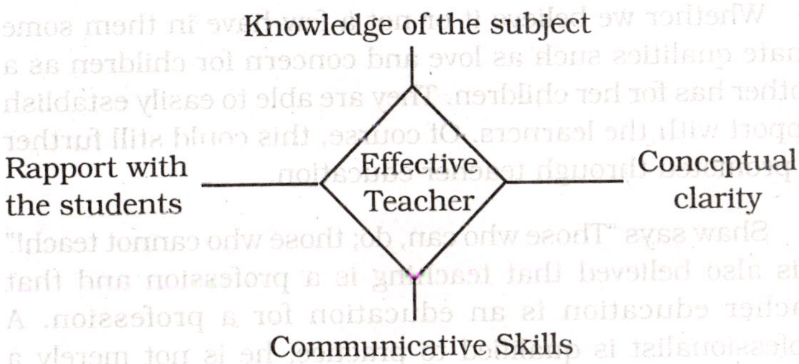

Fig. 3.

Good teachers explain, inform, initiate, direct, administer, unify the group, give security, clarify, diagnose learning problems, prepare curriculum materials, evaluate, record, report, enrich relationship with community, organise classroom activities, participate in all the activities of the institution, and in professional life. Thus, a teacher should ensure an effective and efficient transfer of knowledge. All these can be grouped and explained in the Figure.

Why do we examine the characteristics of teachers and the components of teaching and learning here when we intend to discuss about Teacher Education? Unless we know what we should achieve through teacher education or goal of teacher education we will not be able to provide an effective teacher education programme. Teacher education should aim at developing and promoting the already discussed characters, and competence in teachers.

Teacher Education

Are the teachers born as some say or made? Should the teacher be trained or educated? Should the teachers possess some innate qualities to be teachers? Can we train them to develop the qualities required for teaching? Do the teachers for different levels in the educational ladder require different qualities and abilities? Let us examine all these now.

Whether we believe it or not a few have in them some innate qualities such as love and concern for children as a mother has for her children. They are able to easily establish rapport with the learners. Of course, this could still further be promoted through teacher education.

Shaw says "Those who can, do; those who cannot teach!" It is also believed that teaching is a profession and that teacher education is an education for a profession. A professionalist is qualified to practice; he is not merely a person who possesses knowledge but also directed towards acquisition of certain skills and knowledge required for that particular profession.

There is an urgent need to develop professionalism among teaching community which consists of dedication, sense of belonging, honest academic conduct, awareness about social needs, values, command over the subject matter, genuine interest and concern for students, fellow teachers and the institution in which employed teaching is also a profession which requires keenness, intelligence, practical skills and a high sense of duty and integrity. These are to be inculcated through Teacher education programme.

Teacher as a professionalist uses certain strategies to impart his/her knowledge to others in formal settings such as Pre-schools, Primary schools, Secondary schools, Colleges and in Colleges of Education or Teacher Training Institutes. Teacher education aims at developing and promoting this professionalism in teachers.

We have to evolve a training strategy in Teacher Education to suit their job expectation and performance with emphasis on the basic foundation in Professional knowledge and skills and practices developed on this foundation. They should discover and follow innovative practices in both content and methods; they should not be merely practicing what is existing today. They should go on gaining new knowledge as it is exploding in the field of science and technology. To provide high quality education in 21st Century the teacher should be prepared to acquire new knowledge and the competence to disseminate it. Dynamic youths with high motivation, scientific temper, and excellence in the subject and faith in change should be attracted for teaching careers.

The quality of teachers who have come out of teacher education institutes of any level will depend on the abilities of the students who opted for the teaching profession, institutional climate, the input-instructional materials, methods of teaching and evaluation procedures, followed in the institute guidance and supervision of teaching practice and other practicals, opportunities provided for inculcating values through extra and co-curricular activities and their interaction with the society.

Do we provide all these during the pre-service training of the teachers in the training institutes? Do we give adequate attention to the development f competence through teaching practice and other practical activities in the institutes? Do we expose the teachers under training to the social problems and help them to find the solution? Do we provide them opportunity to realise and cherish the rich cultural heritage of our country? Do we teach them the value system? Do we promote commitments? Do we inspire them to be committed, sincere and efficient teachers? Concentration on these components will strengthen teacher education programme.

Structure of Education in India

"We cannot climb the mountain when the very ground at our feet is crumbling. When the very basis of our structure is shaky, how can we reach the heights, which we have set before ourselves" says Dr. S. Radhakrishnan, a great educationist of 20th century. The structure of education should depict clearly the initial step, the final goal and the duration of each level. Accordingly, the present pattern in India is as follows:

1. Pre-primary stage of 1 to 3 years
2. Primary age of 8 years divided into 2 sub-stages
   (a) Lower Primary stage of 5 years–1st-5th Standard
   (b) Upper Primary or Middle stage of 3 years–6th–8th Standard
3. Lower Secondary or High School–2 years–9th-10th Standard
4. Higher Secondary stage of 2 years-11th & 12th Standard
5. Higher Education stage of 3 years for first degree

Teacher Education should aim at preparing teachers for all these stages and teacher educators for training teachers for different levels.

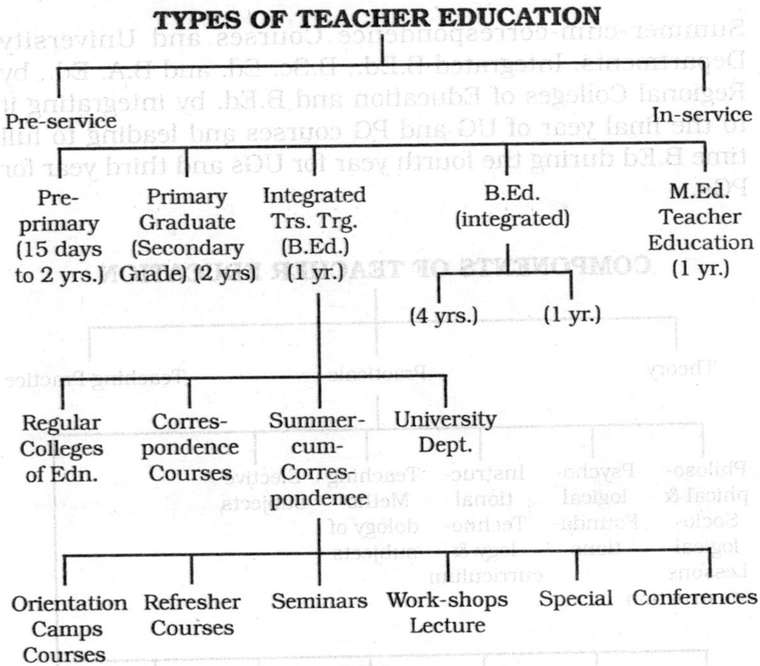

Fig. 4.

Types of Teacher Education

Teacher education can be classified as Pre-service and in service programme. Before recruitment a teacher is expected to undergo the pre-service programme as per the prescribed duration. After an individual joins the profession in order to enrich and refresh the subjects and methods of teaching she is expected to attend the in-service programme periodically.

Pre-service

For teaching at different levels the duration, curriculum requirements, qualification etc., vary, Teacher education is available for Pre-primary, Primary (Secondary Grade), Graduate Teachers Training (B.Ed.) which is being given by Regular Colleges of Education, Correspondence course,

Summer-cum-correspondence Courses and University Departments, Integrated B.Ed., B.Sc. Ed. and B.A. Ed., by Regional Colleges of Education and B.Ed. by integrating it to the final year of UG and PG courses and leading to full time B.Ed during the fourth year for UGs and third year for PGs.

COMPONENTS OF TEACHER EDUCATION

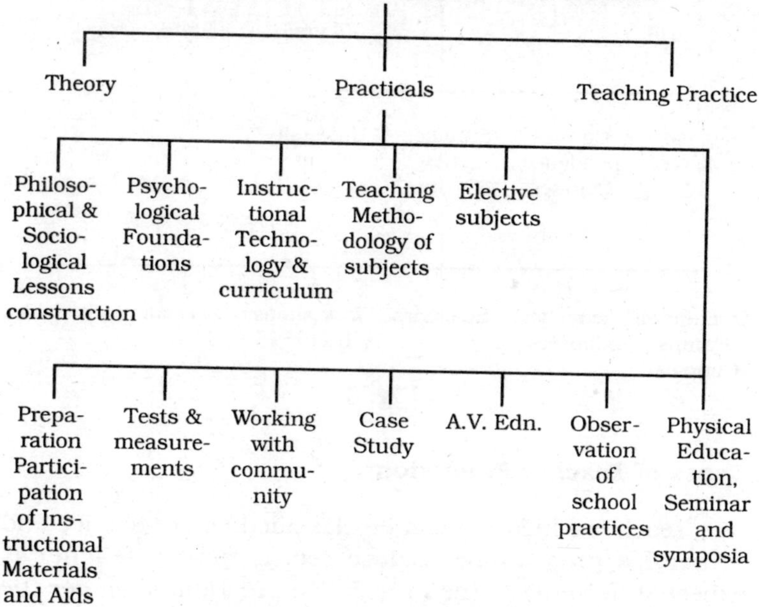

In-service Programme

For the teachers who are in service orientation courses, Refresher courses, Workshops, Seminars, Conferences, Special Lectures and Camps are organised periodically to help them update their knowledge of content and methodology.

Components of Teacher Education

There are three major components in Teacher Education 1. Theory, 2. Teaching Practice, 3. Related Practical activities.

To give the theoretical background to the teacher trainees there are Philosophical and Sociological, Psychological foundation, Instructional Technology Curriculum Construction, Methodology and elective subjects. To face the classroom situation and teach subject of specialisation the teacher trainees are expected to learn the preparation of instructional materials and aids, audio-visual education, tests and measurements, working with community, participation in seminar and symposium, physical education, case study and observation of school practices. They observe the demonstration lessons given by the teachers and peer group. First the trainees learn to teach smaller groups for few minutes and few concepts under micro-teaching sessions.

Practicals-Teaching Practice

Another major component of teacher education programme is teaching practice. The teacher trainees should have a maximum time for developing the art of teaching. At least one-third of the total duration should be utilised for teaching practice. The teacher trainees should properly be guided with regard to the preparation of lesson-plans and instructional materials before they go to the classrooms. Constant supervision and guidance promote the skill in various components of teaching such as stimulus variation, set induction, closure, silence and non-verbal cues, reinforcing students' participation and fluency and methods of asking questions of different types like higher order, divergent etc. They should also be trained in structuring behaviour of feedback in all these components of skill of teaching. Teachers under training should be helped to modify their behaviour and promote teaching competency by giving them the required feedback.

Pre-Primary Teacher Education Programme

The characteristics which are specified and required for teachers especially to those who have to teach the children under five required to be loving and friendly and the ability to establish the link between school and the community.

These personal qualities of the teachers will make the children feel at home when they are away from the home for the first time, in pre-primary school.

Qualification

In India neither Pre-Primary Education nor the Pre-Primary Teacher Education is given importance and recognised by the Government. Hencc, there are more of adhoc and need-based teacher education is learning practiced than a specified form. The trainees who are admitted for pre-primary teacher education possess the qualification, starting from 8th standard pass to the Post-Graduation.

Types

University managed courses like Certificate and Diploma in Pre-school Education and as an optional and as elective at the graduate level.

1. B.Ed. level :- B.Sc., and M.Sc., Home Science with specialisation in Child Development and Pre-school Education.
2. College based programme–where B.Sc., and M.Sc., courses are offered specialising in Child Development and Pre-school Education as an optional and elective at the B.Ed. level.
3. Bala Sevika training–organised by Indian Council for Child Welfare, Department of Social Welfare and Social Welfare Board which are need-based.
4. A few private organisations and community colleges also train the teachers for pre-schools and give certificate.

Duration

The duration of the course ranges from 6 months to 2 years. Usually the certificate courses offered at the university level extends to a period of 6 months to 1 year. In M.Sc., Home Science where the specialisation is child development are expected to undergo teaching at the pre-primary level along with other theoretical back-ground for a period of 2 years. The need-based teacher education programme organised by ICCW Social Welfare Department and Board usually the duration is form 2 months to 1 year.

Curriculum

The trainees are exposed to the theoretical background of Child development/Child psychology, Nutrition and Health and Pre-school education practices and administration. They learn to prepare instructional materials for story-telling, to conduct free conversation, teaching rhymes and creative activities. They observe the children regularly and write a case study, observation of teaching and practice teaching are the major components under practicals. The trainees are assessed for knowledge of the subject matter and the teaching competency.

Secondary Grade Teacher Education

The teachers who teach the Primary School children get the training for a period of 2 years, after a minimum qualification of pass in Higher Secondary examination. Of all the Teacher Education Programme Secondary Grade teachers undergo training for a longer period.

Types

There are two major types of Secondary Grade teacher education Institutes in India: 1. District Institute of Education and Training (DIET), run by Government, and 2. Teacher Training Institute run mainly by private agencies. DIET has come into existence as a result of Educational Policy of 1986 to bring about excellence in education at the primary level. The Government fully supports this training programme. The DIET has very good infrastructure facility with fully qualified teachers for different branches. They organise pre-service programme and also conduct in-service programme in DIET. Teacher training institutes function with minimum staff and minimum facility but follow the same curriculum as it is in DIET. When there was scarcity of secondary grade teachers, the Government introduced Teacher Education Programmes at the Higher Secondary level with the same objective and curriculum, but they no longer exist now.

Curriculum

The courses of study in teacher training institute are grouped into two as Group A and Group B. Under Group A, Educational Psychology and Child Study, Teacher Education and Developing Society, School Management, Teaching of Regional Language, Teaching of English Mathematics, Environmental Studies, Physical, Biological study and Social Studies. Under Group B, teaching practice, preparation of A.V. Aids, Handling of A.V. apparatus, Socially Useful Productive Work (SUPW), working with community, Preparation of Learning Episodes, Health, Hygiene and Physical Education, Project work and Library work are included. Experiences in teaching are provided during both years.

Graduate Teacher Training

Teachers required teaching at the High and the Higher Secondary level are trained at regular colleges of Education for a period of one academic year, and awarded the degree of Bachelor of Education (B.Ed.). Besides this regular programme there are Correspondence Courses, Weekend Courses, Evening Courses and Correspondence-cum-Summer Courses to train the teachers to teach at the High and Higher Secondary School level also existed during late 90s. Usually, the duration of B.Ed. is one academic year under all these schemes. The integrated B.Ed. programme offered by Regional Colleges of Education extends to a period of 4 years to get a degree called B.A. Ed./B.Sc. Ed. Here, the candidate is expected tot learn both content and methodology which means the students have to decide to become the teachers at he time of entering the college.

Curriculum

The curriculum for B.Ed. includes theory and practicals as explained earlier. In Regular Colleges of Education, the trainees have face-to-face contact with the faculty for a minimum period of 180 working days. A periodical and systematic training is given in preparing instructional materials, working with community, SUPW, observation of school practices, Scout and Guide camps and NSS programme. They are supervised by the faculty when they go for teaching practice and give them feed back immediately. This helps the trainees to modify errors if any and develop the right type of teaching competency.

Teaching Practice

Teacher trainees should develop the proficiency in teaching and the techniques of controlling and guiding the students in the classroom. They should be able to translate the theories and principles which they learn into action, for which a considerable attention is to be devoted not only by teaching the theories but how to put them into practice by providing the trainees opportunity to visit the school and test whatever they learn in theory classes, for the possibility of their practicability.

Teacher trainees should be placed in schools at least for about a month to have intensive practice in teaching after observing the experienced teachers' teaching, to observe the activities in the schools in order to understand the multifarious activities of a teacher in a school. First hand experiences alone will make the trainees love the profession and have the commitment along with proficiency in teaching. When the trainees have their internship they develop professionalism by promoting identification, love and honest academic conduct.

Bachelor of Education (B.Ed.) through correspondence, Weekend programmes and Evening Colleges had their own limitations in providing feedback to teacher trainees when they went for teaching practice. As they had few days of direct contact with the faculty, there was less opportunity for them to get guidance from the teachers. Hence the National Council for Teacher Education (NCTE) withdrew the recognition for these programmes.

Master of Education (M.Ed) The prime objective of M.Ed. programme is to prepare the teacher educators who would go and work in Colleges of Education and in the Teacher Training Institutes. But on the contrary, these courses have become attractive to the teaching community in order to get incentive. In the M.Ed. curriculum, they provide theoretical background and orientation to Educational Research through preparation of dissertation.

M.Ed. as Teacher Education programme will become more meaningful if they are given the opportunity to have the teaching practice in the Teacher Training Institutes and in the Colleges of Education. They should be asked to handle the classes and guide the teachers and the training at least for a week.

In-service Programme

Academic Staff Colleges: In the higher education system training in teaching methodology is not emphasized much. Candidates with masters' degree in the concerned discipline are appointed as Lecturers. The New Education Policy of 1986 felt the need for excellence in tertiary education system also. Hence, Academic Staff Colleges attached to nearly 50 Universities in India were started in 1987. The teachers working in colleges were expected to undergo a minimum of one orientation course and two refresher courses for the career advancement. The objectives of the Academic Colleges are as follows:

1. To enable newly appointed teachers to orient themselves with education in general and higher education in particular.

2. To understand the linkage between education, economic, social and cultural development.

3. To acquire basic skills of teaching

4. To understand the role of teachers in achieving national goals

5. To understand the latest development in his/her subject

6. To understand the organisation, management and administration of educational institutions.

7. To utilise the opportunities for the development of personality, initiative and creativity.

The academic staff colleges cater to the needs of teachers working in colleges. Whereas for teachers who are working in High and Higher Secondary Schools, the Institute of Advanced Studies, NCERT, and Regional Colleges of Education provide in-service programme in the form of short-term courses, workshops, seminars etc. For the primary school teachers DIET has taken up the responsibility of providing in-service training periodically.

National Council for Teacher Education (NCTE)

NCTE is a statutory body/organisation which came into existence in 1973. But it did not function as effectively as the Medical Council or the Bar Council or Technical Education Council. But in 1993 an Act (No. 73 of 1993) was passed and in the Preamble it is stated that it should "provide for the establishment of a National Council for Teacher Education with a view to achieve planned and coordinated development of teacher education system throughout the country. The regulation and proper maintenance and norms and standard in the teacher education system and for matters connected therewith."

Functions of the Council

It should be the duty of the Council to take all such steps as it may think fit for ensuring planned and coordinated development of teacher education and for the determination and maintenance of standards for teacher education and for the purposes of performing its functions under this Act, the council may

(a) undertake surveys and studies relating to various aspects of teacher education and publish the result thereof;

(b) make recommendations to the Central and State Governments, Universities, University Grants Commission and recognised institutions in the matter of preparation of suitable plans and programmes in the field of teacher education;

(c) co-ordinate and monitor teacher education and its development in the country;

(d) lay down guidelines in respect of minimum qualifications for a person to be employed as a teacher in schools or in recognised institutions;

(e) lay down norms for any specified category of courses or trainings in teacher education, including the minimum eligibility criteria for admission thereof, and the method of selection of candidates, duration of the course, course contents and mode of curriculum;

(f) lay down guidelines for compliance by recognised institutions, for starting new courses or training, and for providing physical and instructional facilities, staffing pattern and staff qualifications;

(g) lay down standards in respect of examinations leading to teacher education qualifications, criteria for admission to such examinations and schemes of courses or training;

(h) lay down guidelines regarding tuition fees and other fees chargeable by recognised institutions;

(i) promote and conduct innovation and research in various areas of teacher education and disseminate the results thereof;

(j) examine and review periodically the implementation of the norms, guidelines and standards laid down by the council, and to suitably advise the recognised institutions;

(k) evolve suitable performance appraisal systems, norms and mechanisms for enforcing accountability on recognised institutions;

(l) formulate schemes for various levels of teacher education and identify recognised institutions and set up new institutions for teacher development programmes;

(m) take all necessary steps to prevent commercialization of teacher education and

(n) perform such other functions as may be entrusted to it by the Central Government.

NCET/RCTE

SG TE TEI

UNIVERSITY

SG - State Government

RCTE - Regional Committees for Teacher Education

TEI - Teacher Education Institute

If National Council for Teacher Education starts functioning effectively by regularising the norms for starting and granting permission to the teacher training institutes at all levels fixes the qualifications for admission, admission procedures, curriculum, evaluation procedures, we could expect quality in teachers' education. The NCTE through the Regional Committees for Teacher Education and State Governments should monitor the Teacher Training Institutes in the States. Only those Institutes which get recognition and those teacher educators who enroll in NCTE alone should be permitted to train the teachers. These agencies should also have the power to withdraw the recognition and approval if any Teacher Education institutions fail to satisfy the requirements. This could be done through periodical inspection by these organisations. This empowerment will sensitize those who run the Teacher Education institutions as well as teacher educators. It should take care that mediocre and average do not enter the teaching profession.

Emerging Trends in Teacher Education-Future Scenario

When we march towards 21st century demands and expects certain mode of teacher education as the education system itself will get changed to suit the changing trends. Advancement in Science and Technology, Population explosion, awareness of the people for education etc., expect us to modify the strategies of teaching and learning procedures. As we are now eco friendly, we should also accept the inclusion of Environment Education.

Distance Mode of Education

Whether we like it or not distance mode education is gaining momentum with the slogan of "education for all". When we want to provide education for all and every one starts feeling that education is his/her birth right it becomes difficult to provide required number of education institutions. Institution-based form of formal education involves lot of financial commitment and time. Hence, we have to accept the distance education even in Teacher Education with due consideration for promoting the teaching competence and values needed.

Distance education is user friendly. As there is little face-to-face contact in Distance Education we must find a suitable alternative. Contact seminars should be held only in a college of education. Proper use of Mass Media might serve this purpose. Experts with commitment should be permitted to prepare self-learning materials. For taking classes in contact seminars qualified teachers with experience in teacher education with proper preparation alone should be permitted.

Distance education should not be commercialised by admitting large number of people with no motivation to become teachers. Only those who have aptitude for teaching and actually teaching in schools alone should be given admission. Post-graduates and Graduates who think that B.Ed. is another qualification should not be admitted. Adequate facilities should be provided for contact seminars and teaching practice. Teaching practice should not be done in a slipshod manner. Every university should lay down guidelines regarding minimum qualification for admission, norms for each course, facilitates required and tuition fees to be collected by reviewing periodically, enforcing accountability by doing cost benefit analysis.

Suggestions to Improve Teacher Education

NCTE's strong enforcement of its rules and regulations on Teacher Education will strengthen it. Further to this enforcement, mode of training could be based on Task Analysis and Task Performance of teachers. Admission to teacher training should be based on the demand to avoid the problem of unemployment. Best Colleges of Education and Institutes should be chosen to do innovations and research in teaching, learning process. The curriculum for Teacher Education should be modified to be challenging to face the 21st century with advancement in science and technology. Goals of Teacher Education should be reset and curriculum and teaching strategies to be modified accordingly. Qualitative improvement in structure and content will equip the teachers to march towards the advanced world. The emphasis should be not only on teaching face to face but also on software production for mass education through mass media. At the same time Teacher Education should also promote values of modernity of rational and scientific temper, egalitarianism, secularism, freedom and social justice. Teacher Education curriculum should also integrate diversely fulfilled life of human values.

There should be high flexibility in Teacher Education to suit the local needs and culture at the same time maintains a common standard and accountability. Work culture should be encouraged among teachers, with the concern for the learners.

Evaluative tools and procedures in Teacher Education should be modified based on instructional objectives and procedures. Ratio between theory and practical should be worked out and Teacher Education is to emphasize the practical component to make it a competence-based Teacher Education. There should be quality control by monitoring and ensuring minimum infrastructure facilities and human resources in every Teacher Education institution.

Restructuring Teacher Education

On the basis of my 30 years of experience as a teacher educator, the study of existing system of education and a futuristic thinking about education in 21st Century, I would like to offer the following suggestions to improve the teacher education programme.

(a) ***School-linked Teacher Education:*** It is felt that there exists an isolation in teacher education. There is a gap between the producer–the teacher education institutions and the consumer-the schools. Teacher educators have very little contact with the schools, school curriculum and the students. These elements go on changing. But the teacher educators are not aware of these changes.

Teacher educators visit the schools only when the student trainees go for teaching practice, observe their teaching and return to the college.

It is therefore, suggested that every teacher educator should teach at least some units from the subject of specilisation in schools during their leisure hours to familiarize themselves with the requirements of the schools. This close link between schools and colleges of education will pave the way for a meaningful teacher education.

(b) ***Weightage to Theory, Practicals and Practice Teaching:*** There seems to be greater weightage to the theory than to the other two components which promote competence in teaching and bring about attitudinal change. Too much emphasis on theory examination creates a feeling among the teacher trainees to concentrate more on this component and devote very little time on other two components, which are vital to be an effective teacher.

Different techniques and strategies of teaching should be practiced in teacher education so that the trainees get proper models of leading.

Skills needed for teaching should be developed through Micro teaching and Macro level teaching. During practice teaching, teacher educators should supervise at least two classes in the beginning and one at the end of the teaching practice to see the progress and then award the marks or grades.

Similarly before the teaching practice commences, the trainees should be exposed to various practical activities which include preparation of audio-visual aids, instructional materials and methods of using them, techniques of observation of students for case study, test construction etc.

Working with community is one of the practicals in the B.Ed. This has been included in the B.Ed. curriculum to cultivate work culture, concern for society any certain skills required for effective communication and successful living in the society. But this is not followed properly. Care should be taken to make this programme more effective which helps the trainees develop their affective domain and this component will also pave the way for the third dimension of the higher education–i.e. Extension. In fact student trainees be encouraged to adopt a village or a cluster of houses under the leadership of teacher educators to work for total literacy of that particular community. This outreach programme will develop accountability of both teacher educators and the teacher-trainees.

Teachers need to strengthen the base of the freedom, should cope with the challenges of living in a rapidly changing complex world. Teachers have to be prepared, to face new world to come in 21st century with manifold challenges, problems and changes.

Conclusion

If a National level organisation like NCTE with its state level organiztions takes up the issue of Teacher Education the trainees who learn to teach will really learn better to teach. They will also learn when they become teachers to maintain as well as to improve the quality of teaching.

17

Teaching with Devotion

> "We want that education by which character is formed, strength of mind is increased, the intellect is expanded, and by which one can stand on one's own feet"
>
> —***Swami Vivekananda***

Learning is a continuous process from birth to death. The sources of learning, strategies of learning and teaching might differ from time to time but the goals of learning will remain the same. In the context of globalisation, there are changes and challenges in every dimensions of life, including education. The challenges we face as teachers are not only in updating the content or knowledge but also how we disseminate those to the students and how we promote the total development of the young students.

Due to innovations in Science and Technology, the students are highly informative in fact they also have become a challenge to the teachers. Unless a teacher enjoys facing these challenges and takes things with a sportive spirit he/she cannot be in the teaching profession today. Every student with unique Requirement, potentiality, desire, skill etc. will make not only a classroom situation a challenge but even the life outside, as a teacher cannot be just a knowledge provider. Teacher's role in shaping the personality of the student and preparing for a challenging future will be greater outside the classrooms. Teachers, thus to be committed to students and their learning, know the subjects they teach well, proficient in the art of teaching the subjects, responsible for managing and monitoring student, accountable to the society. They should think systematically about their practice and learn from experience, continue to be the learners, and collaborate with other learning committees. What teachers should know and be able to do depends on their perseverance and continuous learning with devotion to the profession.

Engineering is the art of applying scientific and mathematical principles, experiences, judgments and common sense to make things that benefit people. It is a process of producing a technical product or system to meet a specific need of the mass. Engineers have many different types of jobs to choose such as a teacher, a researcher, a designer, builder, an analysist, a producer, a development person, a sales man or a promoter. Each job has a different tasks to be performed. Once an individual discovers his/her desire, aptitude, attitude and capability a choice should be made from among these roles. If any one wants to choose teaching as a profession, he/she should choose it with commitment to the students and the society. Unlike in other jobs in teaching we deal with living, vibrant, energetic individuals who are capable of questioning us. So, a teacher becomes an excellent builder of human beings.

Aims of Teaching

Teaching-learning processes aims at transmission of knowledge, imparting skills and formation of attitudes and values and bring about behaviour modification both in teacher and the taught.

Bloom classifies the taxonomy of educational objectives based on the development of the cognitive, affective and psychomotor domains of an individual. All the three domains should grow in a balanced way to promote an integrated total personality development of the individuals. This has been reiterated by Mahatma Gandhi as the development of

Head, Heart and Hand-3 Hs as the major objective of education. No educationist has said that teaching and learning of Reading, Writing and Arithmetic (3 Rs) alone is the objective of education. To attain the goal of total development of an individual, it is the duty of the teacher to identify appropriate strategy.

Teaching Strategies

When we followed Gurukula System of education it offered multifaceted learning opportunities to the students as they shared the same hut. Whereas today advancement in Science and Technology has made the communication easy and accessibility is very high for learning. Computers, Television, Multimedia, Interactive Television and Networking through computer based electronic message system have become a reality as a learner support system. Shift from print culture to digital technology has affected teaching-learning process and the whole life. Inspite of all these electronic media and other instructional technologies-invading we cannot replace the teacher and the teacher-student instruction in learning and teaching.

Interaction between teacher and student is absolutely essential to develop and promote affective domain and psychomotor domain-the skill development. In the context of making quality education available to all we should also try to make use of instructional technologies to impart effective education to the mass. Educational teaching will help to have maximum output-the learning outcome. Instructional materials could become effective tools only in the efficient and committed teacher. Teachers should develop competence in using these instructional techniques along with concern for the students.

Conclusion

This is my appeal to the teachers/engineers who have chosen teaching profession that you should feel proud of this profession as you are responsible for shaping a teacher, an engineer, a doctor, a professional, an administrator, a politician, a writer, an actor and others who build the nation. You are building and creating a new generation who would in turn will take your message to others.

As a teacher you should know your student first-the client on whom we depend on. Understand his capabilities, interests, attitudes and aptitude along with his background so that you could adjust to him in the classroom and outside. Be a friend, a guide and a philosopher to take him in the right direction.

The second aspect is to know the subject you teach well. Accomplished teachers have a rich understanding of the subjects they teach and establish link with other subjects and relate to life, thus foster their thirst for new knowledge and creative thinking in their students.

Competent and committed teachers command specialised knowledge of how to convey and teach the subject matter to the students. Each subject may have a different strategy of teaching and require different instructional materials. The teachers should be able to understand the effective use of these technologies keeping in mind the students' abilities and the background. The strategies may be multiple in nature.

Teachers are also responsible for managing and monitoring students learning. Teachers should be able to create, enrich, maintain and alter instructional settings to capture and sustain the interests of the students and have most effective use of time. Varied instructional techniques followed by teachers will also help in promoting the learning capacities of the students. Teachers should also know how to engage the individuals as well as group of students to ensure a disciplined, conducive learning atmosphere so as to attain the goal of instruction. Teachers who are committed to the profession will be motivated to encourage the students to be active partners in the teaching and learning process.

Teachers should also get frequent feed back from the students so as to alter, modify and improve the knowledge of the subjects taught and strategies followed in teaching. It will help the teacher to improve his or her knowledge as well as the teaching technology, which is an essential component in helping the students as well as to the teachers. A committed teacher should also be a continuous learner in order to teach the courses effectively. Only a lamp which continues to burn will light another lamp. The accountability of the teachers to the students, the school, the parents and the community would certainly enrich and help professional growth of the teachers.

Teachers with commitment to the profession will certainly remember that their clients-the students-should develop ethical value system so as to be responsible citizens of the society, as the students emulate the teachers. Teachers should be the role models for the students.

By adapting and adjusting to an environmental call, adapting to the educational institution, a teacher can definitely be a contributor to the nation building.

18

Micro Teaching–A Technique of Teacher Preparation

Micro-teaching is a laboratory technique in which the complexities of normal classroom teaching are simplified. Micro-teaching is a scaled down sample of teaching. It is a controlled practice that makes it possible to concentrate on teaching behaviours. The trainee teaches a class of 3 to 5 students. The lesson is reduced a simple concept to five to fifteen minutes and is used for the practice of one particular teaching skill. The lesson is recorded on videotape and the trainee hears and sees herself/himself immediately after the lesson, Or coded by the peer group and the feedback is given to the trainee.

The analysis and suggestions of a supervisor and other sources of feedback assist the trainee in restructuring the lesson. Assessment and feedback lead to further improvements when the she teaches again.

The micro-element is the cardinal feature of micro-teaching which systematically attempts to simplify the complexities of the teaching process. Underlying this is the basic supposition that before one attempts to understand, learn and perform effectively the task of teaching, one should first master the component skills of that task. When one learns to cycle, goes step-by-step learning down. Similarly the different components of skill of teaching is learnt step-by-step, one at a time. Short lessons concentrate on one skill. When the trainee is proficient in this skill, it may be combined with other mastered skills in longer lessons.

Technical Skills of Teaching

A repertoire of teaching skills include skill of stimulus variation, skill of illustrating with examples, skill of introducing a lesson, skill of questioning, skill of explaining, skill of silence and non-verbal cues, skill of using Black-board, Reading, set induction and closure.

Procedures

Usually the following procedures are adopted in Micro-teaching:

1. Planning
2. Teaching
3. Recording or coding
4. Reviewing and Feed back
5. Responding
6. Refining and
7. Redoing

Classification of Teaching Skills

Australian Advisory Committee on Research has classified the teaching skills in the following ways, Motivational skills, presentation and communication skills, Questioning skills, skills of small group and individual instruction, Developing pupil thanking, evaluative skills and class room Management and Discipline.

I. Motivational Skills

1. Giving reinforcement to pupil behaviour
2. Varying the stimulus/Employing variety and variability in teaching
3. Set induction/Using effective introductory procedures.
4. Encouraging a pupil involvement and participation
5. Accepting and supporting pupils' feelings and contributions/Locating and using pupil concerns
6. Displaying warmth and enthusiasm
7. Recognising and meeting children's needs.

II. Presentation and Communication Skills

1. Explaining
2. Dramatising
3. Reading
4. Using audio-visual aids
5. Using effective concluding procedures/closure
6. Employing instructional flexibility/adaptability
7. Clarifying pupil ideas
8. Sustaining pupil ideas
9. Using examples
10. Using silence
11. Verbal and non-verbal cueing
12. Facilitating memorisation

13. Implementing smooth task progression
14. Encouraging pupil-pupil interaction
15. Using pupils' ideas
16. Formulating structuring statements
17. Encouraging pupil feedback
18. Story telling
19. Using non-verbal communication, including
20. non-verbal affective behaviours
21. Using indirect verbal behaviour
22. Lecturing
23. Clarity of presentation
24. Expressiveness
25. Organising the presentation
26. Pacing the presentation
27. Teacher-pupil planning
28. Developing children's oral languages
29. Using planned repetition
30. Ensuring completeness of communication.

III. Questioning Skills

1. Using effective basic questioning techniques (including structuring, posing. Single focusing)

1. Refocusing and redirecting question

2. Using probing questions

3. Using higher-level questions
4. Encouraging and responding to pupils' questions
5. Using convergent and divergent questions
6. Guiding student participation in discussions
7. Asking questions to stimulate pupil initiative
8. Fluency

IV. Skills of Small Group and Individual Instruction

1. Organising small group work/giving small group guidance and supervision.
2. Providing for individual differences through small groups
3. Developing independent learning
4. Individualising instruction
5. Organising independent learning
6. Counseling individual pupil and groups
7. Encouraging co-operative activity in groups
8. Encouraging pupil-pupil interaction in groups

V. Developing Pupil Thinking

1. Fostering inquiry learning
2. Guiding discovery
3. Stimulating creativity
4. Fostering–self –direction
5. guiding pupil learning

6. Developing concepts
7. Using simulation, role-playing and gaming to stimulate thought
8. developing pupil problem-solving skills
9. Encouraging children to evaluate and make judgement
10. Developing critical thinking/increasing critical awareness

VI. Evaluative Skills

1. Recognising and assessing pupil progress
2. Diagnising difficulties
3. Providing remedial measures
4. Encouraging self-evaluation
5. Handling evaluating discussion

VII. Classroom Management and Discipline

1. Recognising attending and non-attending behaviour
2. Supervising class group to secure maximum pupil involvement
3. Displaying task-oriented, businesslike behaviour
4. Displaying awareness of pupil behaviour
5. Giving directions
6. Coping with multiple issues
7. Handling disruptive and unco-ope ive behaviour/ securing classroom control
8. Structuring the classroom environment

9. Establishing the classroom environment
10. Achieving classroom management
11. Encouraging attentive behaviour
12. Maintaining group focus (in contrast to becoming immersed in one child)
13. Maintaining a pupil's orientation to a task.

Stimulus variation includes the following behaviours:

Teacher behaviour	-	Teacher movement
		Teacher gestures
		Change in speech pattern
		Change in sensory focus
		Change in interaction styles pausing silence Oral-visual switching
Pupil behaviour		Pupil movement
		Pupil talk
		Pupil perform
		Pupil gesture

Skill of Stimulus Variation

As it is necessary for a teacher to cxplain, ask questions, give examples, provide encouraging remarks, so also it is important to draw and sustain the attention of the pupils. For this purpose the teacher uses hand gestures, head and body movements, and makes certain verbal statements. Many a time he/she supplements verbal statements with gesture and body movements in order to make it more effective. All these behaviours are related to the skill of stimulus variation.

(i) Movement

The movement of a teacher must have a purpose. That purpose may be to check what pupils at the back are doing or to write something on the black-board or to remove boredom or to sustain attention of pupil who will be observing the teacher standing near the table for a long time. Suppose, a teacher is teaching from the table without moving away from it, this teacher creates boredom in the class or pupils lose their attention in the lesson being taught, since the students are observing him/her continuously for a long time in one place. Suppose, another teacher is continuously walking throughout the class while teaching, this also leads to inattention in pupils. Hence, there must be proper and appropriate movement in teacher.

(ii) Gestures

The various gestures that a teacher can use in the class to draw pupils' attention are head, hand and body movements. Using such gestures, teacher will be more expressive and dynamic in her/his presentation in the class. Gestures can be made by movements of the parts of the body to direct attention, to emphasise importance, to explain emotions, or to indicate shapes, sizes, movements etc.

(iii) Change in speech pattern

To draw an effective attention of the pupils, teacher may change the tone, volume or speed of the speech (including strong emphasis on particular words or pharase) suddenly or radically. These sudden changes in the pitch of the voice will make pupils attend to the idea being told to them.

(iv) Focusing

Teachers, may use some behaviours that direct or focus pupils' attention to a particular point which pupils have to natice or observe. Such behaviours can include.

(i) Verbal Statements (verbal focusing)

(ii) Gestures or movements (gestural focusing)

(iii) Both verbal statements and gestures

(iv) Change in interaction styles:

When two or more persons communicate with each other orally there is said to be oral interaction between them. In classroom, there can be three styles of interaction among pupil and teacher.

(a) Teacher-pupil or teacher-group interaction

(b) Teacher-pupil interaction

(c) Pupil-pupil interaction

(vi) Pausing

In the classroom, if a teacher is continuously talking or asking questions without giving time to pupils to respond, pupils lose their attention in the class. Hence, in order to sustain pupils' attention in the classroom, introduce certain pauses during the teaching and before and after asking question.

Keeping silence in between also attracts the pupils' attention.

(vii) Oral-visual switching

There may be change in the medium i.e. oral, visual, oral-visual through which information is conveyed to the pupils, indicate the change if there is any of the following changes in the media:

(i) Oral = Visual

(ii) Visual = Oral-visual

(iii) Oral = Oral-visual

Skill of Illustrating with Examples

As a teacher, we observe that it is difficult to convey the meanings of abstracts ideas or concepts to children. We must know how to bring clarity, simplicity, and interest in our teaching. The skill of illustrating with examples helps us in this regard.

The skill of illustrating with examples involves two aspects, one related to the formulation of examples used and the other to the way it is presented. Regarding the first aspect of the skill, we must know about the characteristics of a good example. They are (i) it should be simple, (ii) it should be relevant to the concept or rule which it illustrated and (iii) it should be interesting to the pupils.

A simple example is one that is related to the previous knowledge of pupils which can be judged from their participation. An example is said to be relevant to the concept or rule when the concept or rule can be applied to it. An example is said to be interesting if it can arouse curiosity and interest in pupils.

The second aspect of the skill is of presentation by using examples for illustrating. It involves two things– appropriateness of the medium through which examples are presented to pupils and the approaches in presenting the examples. The approach followed in presenting examples involves both the inductive and deductive approaches. The purpose of this skill of illustrating with examples are both to clarify an idea, fact i.e.=dead or rule and to vertify their understanding. For the first purpose inductive approach is followed and for the second deductive approach is employed.

(i) Formulating simple examples

Simple examples is one that is related to the previous knowledge of pupils which can be judged from their participation. The teachers, should try to give examples from the previous concepts, or principle which are clear and understandable to pupils. It is a continuous process. They acquire through many sources like reading books, listening to others, visiting places or getting the first hand experience of situations where many principles are applied.

(ii) Formulating examples relevant to rule or concept

Relevancy of an example to the rule or concept refers to its applicability to the rule or concept which the teacher has to illustrate. Irrelevant examples not only lead to confusion, but also hinder the understanding of the rule or concept which they illustrate.

(iii) Formulating interesting examples

An example is said to be interesting if it can arouse curiosity and interest in pupils. This can be judged by observing the behaviour of the pupils. Examples could be interesting if they are according to the age group and maturity level of the pupils.

(iv) Using appropriate media for examples

To illustrate the examples, the appropriate media like objects, models, pictures, diagrams, maps, sketches, experimental demonstration, are some of the non-verbal and verbal media, that can be used in appropriate places. The term appropriateness refers to the simplicity, suitability to the age level, grade level, maturity level of the pupils and to the unit taught.

(v) Using examples by inductive–deductive approach

Inductive approach involved developing a concept or deriving a rule after giving or electing a number of examples. By this approach, a teacher can easily clarify a concept or rule to pupils. But this approach does not help the teacher to verify whether or not the pupils have understood the concept or rule. For this purpose, deductive approach helps. It involves giving or electing a number of examples after the concept or rule has been stated. Thus, in developing the skill of illustrating with examples, we can follow a combined approach known as inductive-deductive approach:

Inductive approach (Tr. initiates and elicits related examples from pupils' experience to clarify the concept or rule	Stating of the concept or rule (Pupils do this by studying the examples)	Deductive approach (Teacher Elicits examples from pupils to verify their understanding of the concept or rule pupils give their own examples

example→Rule → example

Skill of Introducing a Lesson

When a teacher introduces a lesson or a unit, she/he gives a brief and inspring introduction about the lesson or unit in order to predispose the pupils' minds to it. Generally, an introduction to a lesson includes what the teacher does with or without the help of the pupils upto the stage of stating the aim of the lesson. The teachers differ in the way they introduce a lesson or unit. The pupils' learning of the new lesson or unit largely depends on the way the lesson is introduced. It requires a skill on the part of the teacher to introduce a lesson or unit. The skill of introducing a lesson or unit must involve establishing both cognitive and affective rapport with the pupils. Effectiveness of skill of introduction can be judged by the verbal and non-verbal reactions of the pupils.

The Skill of Introducing a Lesson

In order to develop the skill of introducing a lesson teachers have to practice using more of the desirable behaviours and avoiding the undesirable ones as mentioned below:

Desirable behaviours : a) Using previous knowledge

b) Using appropriate device

Undesirable behaviours : a) Lacking in continuity

b) Uttering irrelevant statements and questions

(a) Using previous knowledge

The previous knowledge refers to appreciative mass or knowledge already possessed by the pupils. They will be acquiring knowledge from various sources like classroom, friends, books etc. If any new knowledge is to be added to this previous knowledge, there should be a logical continuity between them. Using previous knowledge of the pupils while introducing a new lesson must involve bringing the relevant previous knowledge in them to their conscious level.

(b) Using appropriate device

Device refers to the technique that the teacher uses while introducing a lesson. Such devices can be (a) use of examples/analogies/similarities, (b) questioning, (c) explaining lecturing/describing/narrating/illustrating (d) story telling (e) role playing/dramatisation (f) audio visual aids and (g) experimentation/demonstration.

The appropriateness of the use of each of these devices depends on its suitability to the maturity level, age level, grade level, interest, culture, experience of the pupils, and also on the unit to be aught. Although judging the appropriateness of each device is subjective, we can make out by experience those devices such as story telling, role playing/dramatisation, Audio-visual aids the lower classes and the rest to the higher classes. There is no need for rigidity.

(c) Lack in continuity

Continuity refers to the sequence of ideas or information being presented. While introducing a lesson, continuity breaks where statements made or questions asked by the teacher are not logically sequenced. Lack in continuity is there when the teacher's statement or question is not related to the immediately preceding question or statement.

(d) Uttering irrelevant statements or questions

A statement or question, which a teacher utters while introducing a lesson, is said to be irrelevant when it is not related to the aim of the lesson. Such statement or questions do not contribute to the effectiveness of the skill in terms of establishing cognitive and affective rapport with the pupils. Sometimes they may confuse the pupils. While introducing a lesson, there can be continuity but the statement uttered may be irrelevant to the statement of the aim of the lesson.

Skill of Fluency in Questioning

Questioning is an important teaching skills that a teacher must learn. One of the aspects of this skill is the fluency and accuracy in questioning. By fluency in questioning, we mean the rate of meaningful questions asked per unit of time and its correctness. We can say those questions are meaningful which fit in with the issues to be considered under (i) structure (ii) process and (iii) product.

(i) Structure

Structure includes grammatical part and the content part of the question which when taken together convey the intent of the question-maker. Following are the criteria of a well-structured questions (i) grammatical correctness (ii) conciseness (iii) relevance and (iv) specificity.

(i) ***Grammatical Correctness:*** It is desirable that the teacher uses grammatically correct language. If the language used by the teacher is wrong, it will create confusion in the minds of the pupils. So, the teacher should be careful while framing questions.

(ii) ***Conciseness:*** It refers to the length of the question. A question is said to be concise when it does not have redundant or extra words. A question should be direct and straightforward and brief.

(iii) ***Relevancy:*** An irrelevant question is that which is not related to the topic dealt A question is also irrelevant where it contains terms, which are not explained earlier.

(iv) ***Specificity:*** Another criterion for a well-structured question is that it should be specific. A specific question calls for a single answer. It increases the fluency in questioning.

(ii) Process

The word 'process' implies the way of asking questions; the speed of asking question and the voice of the Teacher.

(i) ***Speed of asking questions:*** The teacher should ask out questions neither too hurriedly nor too slowly. If the questions are uttered too slowly, they will decrease the fluency, as it is time consuming and lose track. On the other hand, if the questions are asked too tepidly, and there is no brief pause after the question, then the pupils may find it difficult to follow the questions.

(ii) ***Voice of the Teacher:*** The voice of the teacher should be available and clear to all the pupils in the class. The teacher should put questions in a raised voice in order to enable the pupils to hear the teacher even if they are sitting on the last benches.

Teacher should also repeat the questions for the benefit of slow learners and teachers should also repeat the answers of the students so that others also get the correct answers.

(iii) Product

The term 'product' refers to the pupils' responses. Many a times it happens that nothing is wrong with the structure or the process of the questioning. But even then the pupils do not give any response. Several reasons may be given for such a situation. Some of the important reasons can be enumerated as below:

1. The pupils may not be intelligent enough to understand the questions put to them, or the questions may be of higher difficulty level.

2. Pupils may not bc interested in the lesson. Due to lack of interest, they may be inattentive in the class, hence may not understand the questions.

3. Lack of previous knowledge on the subject may also be responsible for not understanding the questions asked.

4. There may not be any rapport between the pupils and the teacher.

In all such situations, the teacher should re-examine and verify the underlying causes for pupil non-responses to the questions asked.

Sample: Coding Form for the skill of Questioning

In order to understand where the questions asked belong lower order, higher order and their type a form is given. This analysis will help a teacher to improve her/his questioning skill.

		1	2	3	4	5	6	7	8	9	10
Lower Order	1. Prompting										
	2. Seeking further information										
	3. Redirecting										
	4. Refocusing										
	5. Increasing critical awareness										
Higher Order	1. Prompting										
	2. Seeking further information										
	3. Redirecting										
	4. Refocusing										
	5. Increasing critical awareness										

Skill of Probing Questioning

Skill of probing involves going deep into pupil's response by asking a series of subsequent questions. There are five components of the skill of probing questioning. They are:

1. Prompting technique
2. Seeking further information technique
3. Refocusing technique
4. Redirection technique
5. Increasing critical awareness technique

A teacher should understand the reasons for asking probing questions so that she/he could develop that skill:

1. To lead the pupil from 'no' or 'wrong' responses by step-by-step questioning process.
2. To clarify pupil's understanding about the response.
3. To help the pupil to view the response from a broader perspective.
4. To involve more and more pupils in the discussion.
5. To increase critical awareness in the pupils.

The importance of this skill lies in the fact that even though the pupils have given wrong or partially correct response, they are not only given the correct response, but also aware why it was wrong, without resorting to punishment. Secondly, in case of correct response, the pupil is made to examine the response from various viewpoints. Thirdly, this technique increases pupil's critical thinking and their participation in the learning process.

(i) Prompting technique

Prompting technique expects a teacher to give clues or hints to the pupils and ask leading questions. Here, the teacher neither supplies answer to the pupil nor does he/she redirect the question to some other pupils, but helps the pupil to answer the question himself/herself. This technique allows the teacher to probe by prompting the pupil, even though at first instance it appears that pupil cannot answer the question.

Prompting technique can be used by a teacher when the pupil gives (a) I do not know or I am not sure response and (b) very weak or wrong response. Sometimes, it can also be used when the response is partially correct or incomplete, so that pupils understand the correct answer.

(ii) Seeking further information technique

If the initial response of a pupil is either incomplete or partially correct then the teacher helps the pupil to clarify, elaborate, or explain his/her initial response. The teacher elicits more information and meaning or seeks further clarification from the pupil by asking further questions.

(iii) Refocusing technique

This technique is generally used when the pupil gives a correct response and the teacher would like to repeat if for the here fit of the whole class. The teacher related the present answers with the topic already covered in the class. Let us think of a situation in the classroom where there is a pupil who gives a correct response or who has given a high quality response. Here, the teacher refocuses his/her class attention to a related issue. This technique consists of enabling the pupil to review his response in relation to other similar situations. So that they are able to apply in similar situations.

(iv) Redirection technique

Redirection technique involves putting or directing the same question to several pupils for response. This can be used for many purposes. The most important among them are for the purposes of probing and for increasing pupil participation.

(v) Increasing critical awareness technique

This technique mainly involves asking 'how' and 'why' of a completely correct or expected response. The purpose is to seek increased critical awareness in the pupil. The teacher asks the pupil to justify his/he response rationally, through this technique.

Skill of Explaining

Skill of explaining is one of the important skills of teaching. Explaining is to say that it is a process of relating an object, phenomenon, action, or state of affairs to other objects, phenomena, actions or states of affairs so that the understanding about the former is enhanced.

Explaining depends upon the type of past experience of the teacher the type of the new phenomenon and the type or relationships between them.

In a classroom, an explanation is a set of interrelated statements made by the teacher related to a phenomenon, an idea, etc., in order to bring about or increase understanding in the pupils about it.

An explanation will generally be around a phenomenon, action, result, condition, or an event. While giving explanation about any one of them, we will be giving causes for the phenomenon, reasons behind the action, various steps involved in arriving at the particular result, reasons for condition, or various events that have occurred earlier resulting in the event being explained. All such causes, reasons, steps, events, etc., are called antecedents. Such antecedents result in the phenomenon, event, condition, result or action. Each of them is known as a consequent. Thus, an explanation involves giving antecedents to a consequent, which can be diagrammatically represented as follows:

Antecedents (Causes, reasons, actions, steps, events)	Explanation →	Consequent (phenomenon, action, result, event, condition)

Developing the Skill of Explaining

When we get practice to acquire the skill of explaining, the following teacher behaviours have to be developed-using only relevant statements, having continuity in statements, using vocabulary which the pupils know, be fluent in speech, using explaining links, avoiding vague words and phrases, using beginning and concluding statements and testing pupils' understanding by putting a few questions.

Repeating for more clarity, the following are the desirable behaviours, which teachers will practice and develop, and undesirable behaviours, which teaches will avoid in order to develop the skill of explaining:

Desirable behaviours:
- (i) using explaining links;
- (ii) using beginning and concluding statements;
- (iii) testing pupils' understanding.

Undesirable behaviours:
- (i) stating irrelevant statements.
- (ii) lacking in continuity in statements
- (iii) using inappropriate vocabulary
- (iv) lacking in fluency
- (v) using vague words and phrases.

(i) Using explaining links

Explaining links involves using linking words and phrases in the statements of an explanation. Such links make the explanation clearer by bringing continuity in the statements used. They also give a clue that the person is explaining. They are generally conjunctions or prepositions which explicitly indicate the causes, consequences, reasons behind, space sequence, time sequence, means or purposes of an event, concept, action, or condition for example since the red litmus is turning blue, this liquid is an alkali.

(ii) Using beginning and concluding statements

Generally before an explanation certain statements are made for setting the minds of the listeners. Similarly, after the explanation, certain statements are made which conclude the whole explanation. The beginning statements create mental readiness on the part of pupils to listen to what is going to be explained? The concluding statements or summarising statements help in consolidating what has been explained.

(iii) Testing pupils' understanding

This behaviour of the teacher involves putting questions to pupils to test whether or not they have understood what has been explained. Although this may not be a part of explaining, it is essential because it helps in knowing whether the purpose of explaining the concept or phenomenon has been achieved or not.

Undesirable Behaviours

(i) Stating irrelevant statements

While explaining, a statement becomes irrelevant when it is not related to and does not contribute to the understanding of the concept or phenomenon being explained. Such statements not only hinter pupils' understanding, but also distract their attention from the subject of explanation and thus lead to confusion.

(ii) Lack in continuity

The concept lack in continuity refers to break in the sequence of ideas or information presented while explaining a concept. During explaining, continuity breaks in the following situations:

(a) when a statement is not logically related to the previous statement.

(b) when a topic already taught is referred to without showing its relationship with the subject of explanation.

(c) when there is no sequence of place or space.

(d) when there is no sequence of time

(e) when the statements are irrelevant

(iii) Using inappropriate vocabulary

Use of inappropriate vocabulary involves using terms unknown to most of the pupils of that age group and grade level. Although it is difficult to decide the appropriateness of the vocabulary to be used, we can do it by experience. This involves subjective judgement. Sometimes, more difficult technical terms are used to explain certain simpler terms. Sometimes almost all the technical terms used in an explanation may not be appropriate for the particular class or age group. If we are aware of the contents and sequences of the contents in the prescribed textbook for that particular class, it will not be difficult for us to find out the inappropriate vocabulary.

(iv) Lacking in fluency

Lacking in fluency is revealed when a teacher speaks incoherently. There is a lack in fluency when a teacher speaks half sentences or reformulates in the midway of a sentence or a statement. When there is lack in fluency, it not only distracts pupils' attention from what is being explained, but also hinders their understanding of the subject of explanation. They also lose the continuity.

(v) Using vague words and phrases

Sometimes while explaining teacher uses such words and phrases which are vague indicate that he is failing to make something explicit. The use of such words and phrases hinders the understanding of what is being explained.

Skill of Silence and Nonverbal Cues

To attract the pupils the teacher should also be silent and use non-verbal cues some time in the class room. Let us see the behaviours included in the skill of silence and non-verbal cues by defining the two key words, namely, silence and nonverbal cues. Silence means pause, teacher remains silent without speaking means pause, teacher remains silent without speaking anything, thus gives pupils a chance to think and be curious. Non-verbal cues include those behaviours that convey meaning without words, like facial cues, body movements, head movements and other movements in the class.

Silence

Silence is an effective teaching tool in order to make pupils participate. It involves pupils in classroom interaction. Often in teaching, teachers are not aware of usefulness of silence. In an instructional sequence, a teacher should give a pause for a few seconds before calling out a pupil. Although the pause time cannot be fixed, depending upon the length of the pupil response, the nature of pupils, etc., length of pause can be divided. Pausing behaviour eventually comes to serve a two-fold function: (i) it provides a discussion atmosphere and (ii) it also helps pupils in learning to use pause to organise a more complete answer.

Non-verbal cues:- Facial cues

Facial cues are the easiest one to recognise the mood of the teacher and they form one of the most powerful means of communications. For a teacher, they are one of the most useful means of communications, because most of time pupils' attention is mostly focused on the teacher's. Different types of facial cues are used for different purposes. A smile directed towards a responding pupil encourages him to answer. A frown, from the teacher indicated displeasure with the pupil's response. Looking thoughtfully as the pupil's responds, indicates that, the teacher is seriously considering the response. Continuing to look seriously at the pupil while he is responding which usualy encourages him to continue talking and indicates that the teacher is giving thought to the pupil's answer and looking quizzically at the pupil as though his answers were not clear usually stimulated the pupil to revise his answer and elaborate upon it.

Head movements

Nodding the head helps a lot in reducing the teacher talk. A node by the teacher will indicate whether or not the response is correct. It will also indicate to the pupil whether or not he is on the right track.

To conclude, Micro-teaching is an important component and technique in teacher education programme. As prompting/developing skill of teaching is the major objector of teacher education opportunity is given to the trainees to learn and practice different components of teaching stage by stage in the training institute itself before they really face a group of students in a class room situation. Micro teaching practice promotes self confidence in teaching and the teacher trainees learn various skills under the able guidance of an experienced teacher. Feed back given by both the teacher and the peer group helps the trainees modify their teaching strategy. Micro teaching grooms the young students to be effective teachers in the class room.

19

Systems Approach in Education

The exploding population, the expectation explosion, the rate at which new knowledge is being generated and the changing technology of the society are the four major factors which demand that education should wed itself to science and technology, and develop the capacity to adapt to new technology of teaching and manage change. This has led to search for an eductional technology. The strategy of teaching is therefore today entering a period of revolution. The National Council for Educational Technology of U.K. has defined Educational Technology as "The development, application and evaluation of systems, techniques and aids to improve the total process of learning." In Nutshell, systems approach states that education means "certain inputs" (books, teachers, activities etc.) which are processed to produce some change in behaviour of learner (learning).

The instructional process has become so complex these days, in terms of the amount of material to be taught, the media to be utilised and strategies and number of students and teachers involved in teaching and learning process. In such a situation, there is great need for comprehensive understanding and detailed planning. The curriculum should not only specify student behavioural objectives but also suggest the strategies for helping the students to reach the objectives/goals and evaluation instruments to measure their success. This is called the System Approach, as operational planning concept, borrowed from the engineering science and cybernetics, which deals with self-regulating and self-sustaining systems.

The problems in the field of education are very complex as the process of education involves human beings-students, teachers, parents, educationists, administrators, and other members of the community. To deal effectively with the various problems in education, and to plan the necessary programmes, the complexity of the situation should first be properly analysed. Any problem in the field of education would have multiple causes, and the solution of the problem would call for the consideration of several variable. Such a complexity lends itself to systems approach, which deals with self regulating and self sustaining systems in solving problems.

System analysis helps us in understanding better the various components of the system and the various interactions between them, which in turn enables us to identify weak spots in the system and control it effectively so as to produce the desired results for which it has been designed.

"Education like many other professions has its researchers and operators. But what education does not have is the engineers who translate research into improved operations." (Charles, L.Wales, 1970). The design of an educational system is the area in which this engineer can make the most significant contributions. It is in the hands of the teachers who are the social engineers become the system operators.

Systems approach is a technique that gives much promise when applied to education through which a thorough analysis of a system/subsystems of teaching learning and evaluation procedures could be effectively carried out.

System approach is a genetic term that provides a body of theory and practice. System movement aids in improving the practice of educational curriculum planning, instructions, evaluation and administration.

System approach in education is an inter-disciplinary one, which provides a framework within which, many separate and possible divergent distribution to the overall optimisation of the problem or issue, could be worked out.

It is, the organisation of a process consisting interrelated parts designed to transform a certain input for its environment into an output designed by the environment. Interrelation among various components enables every one do his/her job relation to the total objectives of the system and execute his/her own part.

System approach helps in improving the quality and quantity of the output of the system. It is a systematic way of identifying the goals and scientifically working out different steps and stages to achieve the goals.

Definitions

A system is "A group of objects related or interacting so as to form unity". It also defines a system as "organised or established procedures", or "a methodically arranged set of ideas, principles, methods or procedure".

The term systems approach, system analysis or systems procedure are used in literature at various levels of sophistication. At a layman's level, they indicate systematic thinking, step-by-step problem solving and considering many variables not in isolation of each other but as interacting with each other-studying the phenomenon or process as whole and not in bits and pieces.

The term 'system' is used in many contexts in human body. For example we discuss the circulatory system and nervous system. In daily life we encounter political system, communication system and many others. In all contexts, the word system denotes an assemblage of components.

The Webster's Dictionary defines a system as "an assemblage of objects united by some sort of regular interaction and inter-dependence". "A system is a group of objects related or interacting so as to form an unity."

System is the process taken as a whole incorporating all its aspects and parts namely pupils, teachers, curriculum, content, instructional materials, institutional strategy, physical environment, the evaluation, administration etc. Hence, the purpose of the system approach is to get the best equipment in the best place for the best people at the best time and at the best price." It is a scientific and rational method of optimising the outcomes of a system by making the best possible utilisation of existing and anticipated resources.

Systems Approach: The Concepts

According to Banathy (1972) systems approach to instruction has been defined as "systematic way of analysing a problem and solving it". In other words it is a way of systematically analysing how every aspect of an instructional problem is inter related and interact with each other.

Twelker etal (1972) describe the system approach as a management tool that allows individuals to examine all aspects of a problem to interrelate the effects of one set of decisions to another and to optionally use the resources at hand to solve the problem.

Deaden (1972) says that "systems approach is nothing more or less than what a competent, smart, adequate business executive adopts in the ordinary conduct of his business". According to him systems approach is merely the ancient art of management as performed by competent managers. After giving this general view and referring to many definition of systems approach given by other scholars, he selects a representative definition given by Maridakis (1971) with which he agrees. Maridakis says the systems approach to management is basically a way of thinking. The organisation is viewed as an integrated complex of interdependent parts which are capable of sensitive and accurate interaction among themselves and with their environment.

The chief attribute of system approach is that it can be applied with equal effectiveness to problems of a material nature with well defined boundaries as to the very process of delineating the boundaries of a dilemma so that it can be focused sharply into a problem and then be solved. It does imply that the system approach is not only successful in problem solving but also in locating actual boundaries of problem and its environment.

In education, system approach is a rational problem solving method of analysing the educational process and making it more effective. System is the process taken as a whole incorporating curriculum content, instructional content, instructional materials, instructional strategy, physical environment and the evaluation of instructional objectives. Hence it may be seen that the purpose of the systems analysis is to get the best equipment in the best place for the best people at the best time and at the best place.

Characteristics of a System

Each system must possess the following characteristics for an effective functioning:

(i) It should have a clearly identifiable structure or organisation.

(ii) The structure must be orderly and must have some component parts.

(iii) It should be possible to identify the parts clearly in relation to each other and in relation to the whole.

(iv) It must have integrity, i.e., all the components contribute to a common purpose.

(v) A change in one variable of the system produces corresponding changes in the other variables.

(vi) It must be stable, controllable and observable.

Components of an Instructional System

System approach is a systematic attempt to co-ordinate all aspects of a problem toward specific objectives. In education this means, planned and organised use of all available learning resources, including audio-visual media, to achieve the desirable learning objective by the most efficient means possible.

The systems approach focuses first upon the learner and the performance required of him only then makes decisions regarding the course content, learning experiences and the most effective media and instructional strategies. Such a system incorporates within itself the capacity of providing continuous self correction and improvement. Its purpose is to ensure that the components of the organic whole will be available with the proper characteristics, at the proper time to contribute to the total system fulfilling the objectives.

The Procedural Steps in the System Approach in Education

1. Defining instructional goals in terms of the behavioural objectives.

2. Determining functions related to the achievements of these goals by proper aids like films, recording, video tapes etc.

3. Defining learner characteristics and requirements.

4. Choosing appropriate methods suitable for effective learning of the topic.

5. Selecting appropriate learning experiences.

6. Selecting appropriate materials, facilities equipment, resources, environment and tools required for student experiences.

7. Defining and assigning roles-teacher-team-teaching members and–supporting students.

8. Implementing the Programme.

9. Testing and evaluating the outcome in terms of original objectives measured in student performance.

10. Refining and revising if necessary to improve production and efficiency of the system to improve student learning.

In an instructional system, the teacher or instructor and the resources made use of by him are included as components of the system. In the systems approach to instruction, the teacher has to plan completely the utilisation of selected resource material and the classroom activities. The teacher should have an overall view of the subjects, know his/her limitations, know all about his/her pupils and individual differences in their learning capacities and plan accordingly. The systems approach involves continuous evaluation of learning outcomes, and utilisation of knowledge gained by analysis of results of evaluation to suitably modify the plan of approach to achieve the stated objectives.

In this elementary form, the education system can be represented as follows.

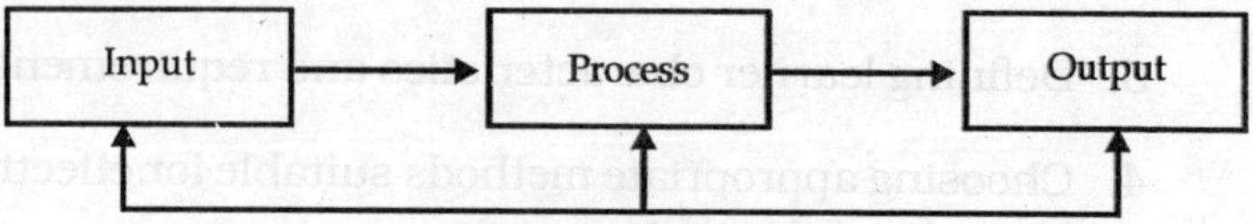

Fig. 1.

In an instructional system, the teacher or instructor and resources made use of by him/her are included as components of the system. The teacher can apply the systems approach in the instructional process, for effective transaction of the curriculum.

Planned input and processes involving structural learning materials and methods in the form of learners development are suitably geared to the needs of a particular group of learners. Monitored output is used to revise the content and methods, improve and evaluate the instructional system, provide feedback to the learner and teacher and a degree of in-put flexibility to adjust to individual situations.

The parts of the instructional system noted can be analysed into their possible components as follows:

I. **Input** – The students—age

— minimum prescribed entry qualification attainments

— their attitude and aptitude

— job opportunities avilable after passing out

— location of the institute–rural/urban

— Economic background

— Social status

— facilities available

— cost involved.

II. **Process:** The teaching –learning process–need based.

(i) Curriculum— well defined objectives with anticipated behavioural outcome, changes expected in students.

— suggested teaching method and media

— evaluation procedures laid out.

(ii) Institute — physical environment

— location

— buildings, classrooms, equipment,

— library

— other facilities

— teachers–professional qualification or training- experience–altitude and efficiency.

(iii) Output — students passing out of the Institute with recognised qualification and attainment as required quality, knowledge and skills-in case of production–a desired amount and quality.

(iv) Feedback — evaluation–by public organisations–the students-customers internal, external, boards, universities.

— periodical evaluation or terminal examination will reveal the success or failure of the teaching –learning process.

— The teacher compares the performance of his student at each stage with laid out criteria and modifies the instructional procedures according to requirement.

For maximum effectiveness in teaching, learning process it is necessary to consider the system as a whole remembering the interaction and inter-dependence of the components of the system. System approach in education may be applied to institutional planning and development in its varied aspects (macro level) or it may be used at the classroom level with its concern of a specified topic during a brief period (micro level).

In administrative decision making situation, the input consists of problem or issues, data and alternatives, which must be operated on, as well as proper, analysis of evaluation procedures and thought processes which operate.

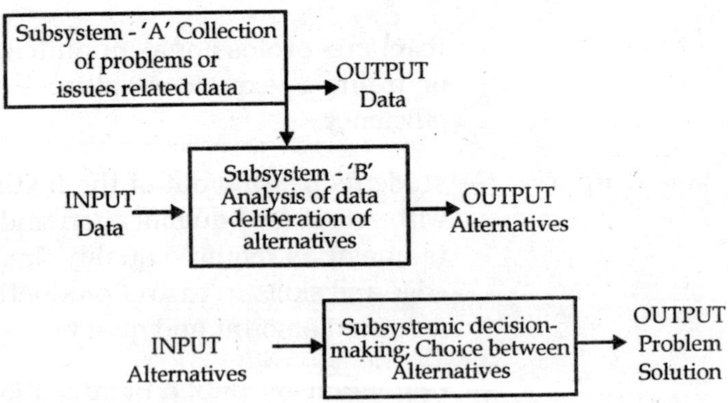

Fig. 2.

Through system approach in education we could improve the stating of objectives, teaching and testing, as given in the Fig. 3.

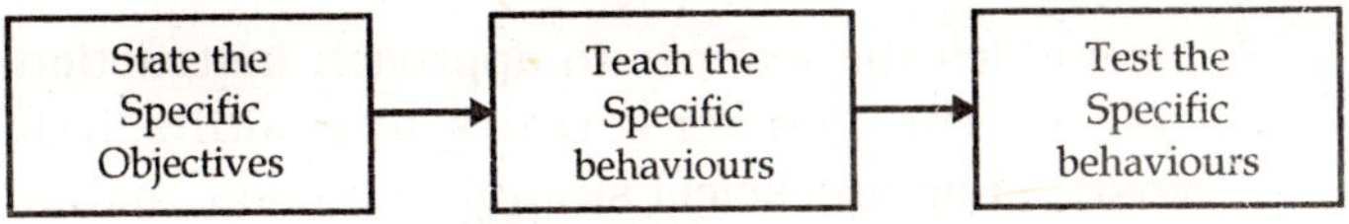

Fig. 3.

In every system there are subsystems whether school or society or a body. In an organisational system like school there are important functional subsystems such goals, work or action, communication and monitoring. All these subsystems contribute in a vital way to the inter-relationship of subsystem activity and to overall system input-output linkage.

Advantages of System Approach to Education

1. Provides conceptual framework towards a set goal.
2. It helps to identify the suitability or otherwise of the resource material to achieve the specific goal.
3. It helps to assess the resource needs, their sources and facilities in relation to quantities, time and other factors.
4. Technological advance could be used to provide integration of machines, media and people for attaining the defined goal.
5. It permits an orderly introduction of components required for systems success in terms of student learning.
6. Rigidity in plan of action is avoided as continuous evaluation affords feedback to more towards desired beneficial changes to be made.
7. Systems approach to instruction enables the teacher to analyse the teaching leaning process in a systematic way.

8. It enables the teacher to approach instruction to assess the learner's traits and skills before instruction and select suitable methods, materials and media of instruction.

9. It enables the teacher to evaluate the learner's outcome and to continue revision until a presented level of achievement is reached or until the objectives themselves change.

10. It enables the teacher to pre-specify the goals of instruction and process of instruction.

The spirit of this systems Approach advocated by technology is what is being reflected in educational technology too. Its ultimate goal is development of the nation for which productivity at all levels has to be ensured. This could be made possible only by maintaining the spirit of the systems approach in all aspects of education.

20

Taxonomy of Educational Objectives

Process of education begins with statement of objectives, which leads to choosing appropriate teaching–learning strategies and thereafter deciding means to evaluate attainment of these objectives. This means objectives decide the teaching strategy and evaluation.

The idea of classification system of educational objective was formed at an informal meeting of college examiners who attended the 1948 American Psychological association convention in Boston. A committee headed by Bloom–a psychologist was assigned the task of organising and writing Taxonomy of Educational objectives. The main purpose of constructing a taxonomy of educational objectives was to facilitate communication method of improving and exchange of ideas and materials among examiners, as well as other persons concerned with educational research and curriculum development.

Taxonomy of educational objectives is basically a classification scheme. Taxonomy is of extremely useful guide to develop a comprehensive list of instructional objectives, in education on teaching, learning and evaluation, is called Taxonomy of educational objectives.

Objectives are specific purposes formulated for teaching as well as for testing student's achievement. The objectives are stated in the form of behaviour modification in students. It has two parts, one part describes the kind of change or modification to be brought about in the student and the second part describes the kind of content through which the modification is to be brought out. The first part may be called the modification part and the second one the content part. This taxonomy is not designed in terms of teacher behaviours or instructional methods.

Learning objectives can be divided into three basic categories (i) objectives related to development of knowledge, (ii) objectives related to inculcation of attitudes and (iii) objectives related to doing skill development.

In order to explain the major three aspects of behaviours changes-intellectual, emotional and physical, Bloom identified the following three major domains of objectives Cognitive, Affective and Psychomotor, arranged from simple to complex on the basis of level of complexity or difficulty.

Cognitive Domain

Objectives relating to cognitive domain includes those objectives that deal with knowing, thinking and problem-solving and the development of intellectual abilities and skills. This domain contains six major classes of objectives arranged in an hierarchical order on the basis of the complexity of the task; and they are arranged also from 'simple' to complex behaviour such as (1) knowledge, (2) comprehension, (3) application, (4) analysis, (5) synthesis and (6) evaluation.

(i) Knowledge

Knowledge as per Bloom's taxonomy includes those behaviours and test situations which emphasis remembering, either by recognition or recall of ideas, materials or phenomena. The behaviour expected of the student in a recall situation is very similar to the behaviour he would have had during the original learning situation. In this learning situation the student is expected to store in his mind certain information and remember and recall at a later stage when expected without any alteration. As per this definition, knowledge is split into six types as given under:

1. Knowledge of specified recall of specific and isolated bits of information;
2. Knowledge of terminology or reference for specific verbal and non verbal symbols;
3. Knowledge of trends and sequences of the processes, directions and movements of phenomena with respect to time;
4. Knowledge of specific facts of dates, events, persons, places sources of information etc.;
5. Knowledge of criteria by which facts, principles, techniques and procedures are employed in a specific areas; Knowledge of theories and structures of the body of principles and generalisations, together with inter relations which presents clear, and systematic complex phenomenon or fields.

(ii) Comprehension

Comprehension is defined as the ability to grasp the meaning of the materials presented. It represents the lower level of understanding and includes skills such as translation, interpretation and extrapolations. Translation is the comprehension as evidenced by the care and accuracy with which the communication is rendered from one language to another. And interpretation is the explanation or summarisation of a communication. Extrapolation is the extension of tendencies beyond the given data to determine the consequences or effect.

(iii) Application

It is the ability to use the learned materials in new situations. Learning outcomes in this area require a higher level of understanding than those under comprehension. It demands use of ales tractions in particular situations. The altrations may be in the form of idea, rules or generalised methods.

(iv) Analysis

It refers to the ability to break down the given material into its component parts so that the organisation of its structure may be understood. Learning outcomes here represent a higher intellectual level than comprehension and application, because they require an understanding of both the content and the structural form of the materials. This includes an analysis of elements, relationships and organised principles.

(v) Synthesis

This refers to the ability to put together elements and parts so as to form a new whole-learning outcomes in this area stress creative behaviours with major emphasis on the formulation of new pattern of a structure. This includes the production of a unique communication or a plan or proposed set of operations and derivation of a set of abstract relations. In otherwords, it is pushing together of elements or parts so as to form a whole, i.e., arranging and combining them to constitute a structure which was not clear before.

(vi) Evaluation

This is concerned with the ability to judge the value of given materials, statements, novels, poems and research, reports. The judgements are to be based on different criteria. This includes judgements in terms of internal evidence and of external criteria. It is quantitative and quantitative judgements about the values material and method for given purpose judgement may be in terms of internal or external criteria.

A list of associated action verbs for stating cognitive domain has been provided here under:

Objectives	*Associated Action Verbs*		
Knowledge	Define	Write	Underline
	State	Recall	Select
	List	Recognise	Reproduce
	Name	Label	Measure
Comprehension	Identify	Illustrate	Explain
	Justify	Represent	Judge
	Select	Name	Contract
	Indicate	Formulate	Classify
Application	Predict	Choose	Construct
	Select	Find	Compute
	Assess	Show	Use
	Explain	Demonstrate	Perform
Analysis	Analyse	Select	Justify
	Identify	Separate	Resolve
	Conclude	Compare	Break-down
	Differentiate	Contrast	Criticize
Synthesis	Combine	Argue	Select
	Restate	Discuss	Relate
	Summarize	Organize	Generalise
	Precise	Derive	Include
Evaluation	Judge	Support	Identify
	Evaluate	Defend	Avoid
	Determine	Attact	Select
	Recognise	Criticise	Choose

Stating the Behavioural Objectives of Cognitive Domain

In describing the behaviour that is required for student whn he/she demonstrates his/her mastery over the subject or the skill, it is important to identify, in a very clear terms, exactly what will he/she do. This involves saying how will he/she recognise the one or situation which will cause him/her to commence action or behaviour, as well as how will he recognise that the action has been successfully accomplished.

These action verbs should be used for defining the educational objectives of cognitive domain and also for examination questions.

So if a teacher has a thorough knowledge of Bloom's taxonomy of cognitive educational objectives with the associated action verbs it will be more useful to identify the meaningful level at which the learner is working.

Affective Domain

Affective domain includes those objectives, which describe some feeling or emotion. It also includes those, which deal with interests, attitudes, appreciations and values.

It is divided into five major classes arranged in an hierarchical order arranged a iong a continuum of internalisation lowest to highest.

(i) Receiving: (attending)

Receiving means that the learner must be sensitized to the existence of certain phenomena, and stimuli. This includes awareness and willingness to receive controlled or selected emotions.

(ii) Responding

Responding is concerned with responses that go beyond merely attending to phenomena. A person is actively involved in attending to them. This includes acquaintance in responding, willingness to respond and satisfaction in response.

(iii) Valuing

Valuing includes acceptance of a value preference for value and commitment to or a conviction in regard to a certain point of view.

(iv) Organisation

In situations where there are more than one value is relevant, there is a need for (a) the organisation of the values into a system. (b) the determination of the inter relationships among them (c) and the establishment of the domain and pervasive value. It includes conceptualisation of values and organisation of a value system.

(v) Characterisation

Characterisation is the ability to conceptualise a value to organise its interrelationship and values into a total philosophy. It is a basic orientation, which enables the individual to reduce and order the complex world about him/her and to act consistently and effectively in it.

Psychomotor: Domain

Blooms and his associates have not developed classification of educational objects under Psychomotor domain. But many taxonomies have been developed by Ragsdale, Guilford, Dave, Kibler and Harrow.

The categories of Harrow's taxonomy and the relevant behavioural terms are given below:

Objectives		*Associated action verbs*
1. Reflex movements	:	respond, react, run
2. Basic fundamental movements	:	walk, move, jump
3. Perceptual abilities	:	discriminate, select, separate
4. Physical abilities	:	hold, adopt, continue
5. Skilled movements	:	manipulate, sing, dance
6. Non-discursive communication	:	gesture, use of non-verbal cues, understand non-verbal messages.

Psychomotor domain includes those objectives which deal with manual and motor skills. This is based on the concept of co-ordination between various muscular actions. Behaviours which include muscular actions require neuro-muscular co-ordination. These muscular activities are grouped under psychomotor domain. The job of the teacher is to provide such activities that may help to develop neuro-muscular co-ordination. These objectives are most frequently related to handwriting and speech, physical education, trade and technical courses, in which hands on experiences are involved.

The educational objectives tentatively proposed under this domain of Psychomotor are:

(i) perception: perceiving a skill being performed by someone,

(ii) imitation of an action or some performances or activities,

(iii) manipulation of an act, which includes differentiating among various movements and selecting the proper one,

(iv) precision ; in reproducing a given act, which helps accuracy proportion and exactness in performance,

(v) articulation among different acts, which includes co-ordination sequence and harmony among acts,

(vi) naturalisation, where a pupil's skill attains its highest level of proficiency in performing and acting with the least expenditure of psychic energy. The act becomes so automatic that it is attended unconsciously.

Compared to cognitive and affective domain, very little work has been undertaken in the classification of educational objectives under psychomotor domain.

Kinds of Behaviours

Behaviour of a pupil is governed by his development in three domains–cognitive, affective and psychomotor. The cognitive domain is mainly concerned with the ability of a student to do a task, while the affective is willingness to do that task. The psychomotor domain deals with the actual performance of a task.

Cognitive behaviour relates to thinking, understanding judging and other intellectual behaviours. This kind of behaviour is internal or covert behaviours and there are corresponding external or overt behaviours from which we can infet the covert behaviours that should have led to the overt (external) behaviours.

We speak, we play, we run, we write, we do so many activities which are known as psychomotor behaviours. They are psycho (mind) because we have to think before we act and they are motor because they involve movement. We have so far discussed about two types of behaviours. They are the cognitive behaviour and the psychomotor behaviour. Apart from these two types of behaviours, there is another type of human behaviour. Of course, we think, we do, we feel also. Sometimes we feel happy at times we are sad; we love; we are affectionate to others, angry etc. This feeling behaviour is known as affective behaviour. Affective behaviour, like cognitive behaviour, is convert, internal; but we can infer that from the psychomotor behaviours of the individuals.

Analysis of Cognitive Behaviour

There are six levels of objectives of cognitive behaviour. The first level is simple knowing. It is mere awareness of something. Then comes understanding. We know that understanding is different from knowing. So to understand something, we have to know it and also know more about it. Understanding therefore, is the higher level of thinking than mere knowing.

If we have a clear understanding about a thing or an idea, what it is, how it is related to other things or ideas, and how it can be used, then we think of using that thing or idea in different ways in different situations. We think of applying that idea to solve new problems. We teach our students 'heat expands bodies'. Now here is our Sarojitha. She hears what we tell and becomes aware (knows) of the idea / the concept. Then her understanding will expand. One day she has to fill her fountain pen with ink. She tries hard but she is not able to unscrew the neck of the pen. She thinks and thinks and remembers that heat expands bodies, the idea/concept she has learnt and understood before. Now she thinks of using this idea to solve her problem, namely, how to unscrew the neck of the pen. She tries this she heats the neck of the pen and the neck unscrews easily. She has applied the idea/concept, 'heat expands bodies' to solve her problem of unscrewing the neck of the pen. This level of thinking, that is, thinking to apply an idea or principle that is known and understood to solve a problem is a content different from that in which it is "learnt". It is the application of cognitive ability. The application ability requires the ability of understanding and this ability requires in turn the knowledge.

Bloom identifies three more higher level of thinking or cognitive abilities. They are analysis, synthesis and evaluation. Suppose I read a couplet from Thiru Kural, you hear it and then try to understand it. You break the couplet into meaningful parts and try to understand how these parts are to give the meaning the couplet conveys. This way of understanding requires a higher thinking ability. This higher level of understanding requires breaking down something (the Kural couplet) into its constituent parts and understanding the relationship among the parts is called the analysis–the ability to analyse.

Suppose I ask you to tell me something about your experiences, what will you do? You recall your experiences, arrange them in a sequence and then narrate your experiences. Your thinking requires recalling events, arranging and combining and sequencing them to present a whole narration. This cognitive ability is named the ability to synthesis.

We have to select students for awarding prizes. Five students have composed poems. Now we have to select two students for the prizes. How are we going to select two students for the prizes? We judge, we evaluate their poems and if they are upto the standard, then we award prizes. We make judgement about the extent to which their poems satisfy the standard. This ability to compare a work with known standards is called evaluation ability. Evaluation is the highest cognitive ability in Bloom's hierarchy.

Analysis of Affective Behaviour

Affective behaviour deals with feelings and attitudes. How do we develop affection towards something or somebody. Last month one day Gokul saw a puppy. It came near him. When it came near him, he looked at it. He received the visual stimuli that the little dog presented. His affection towards that animal started with this receiving of the sight. Then he made some noise (itch so itcho') to call the puppy near him that little animal responded to the sound and came near him. When it came near him he touched it, moved his hand over its back softly. He also responded to the dog's coming near him. First he received and then responded to the stimuli from the puppy. Gokul somehow did not like to spend time playing with it. He liked to spend more time with the puppy than with the lamb. He valued spending time, playing with the puppy more than spending time with the lamb. So he spent more time receiving and to responding to dog and also valuing this responding more than the responding to any other puppy or lamb or animal.

Gokul spent time playing with the puppy, father did not scold him; but he encouraged him and told him that he should develop affection towards all animals, not only with that particular puppy. Gokul values that his preference to spend time with the puppy did not go contrary to the values of father other members of the family or even to the values he had developed already. You know Gokul likes reading English very much. He values English, but the puppy did not take much of his time not allowing him to read English. The puppy value (that is his liking to spend time with him) suited well with his other value such as reading English and obedience to elders. This value got organised with other values. The affective behaviour at this level is organisation.

If both the values get well organised, then he continues reading English and playing with the puppy and derives pleasure from both. Then it becomes his habit, his usual behaviour, his characteristic way of behaviours. Affection to the dog now becomes a characteristic behaviour of Gokul.

Analysis of Psychomotor Behaviour

The third domain of our behaviour is the psychomotor domain, skill development is the concern of this behaviour. Let us analyse a psychomotor behaviour and try to understand the objectives.

First Lalith saw some one going on a bicycle. This is perceiving. Then he got a bicycle and tried to ride on it. He imitated the cyclist. Some one helped him to sit on the seat; he had seen, perceived what those who rode on cycles did. So he tried to-do what they (cyclist) 'generally do'. He imitated them. He is a little bit successful. He balanced on the seat, pedaled, managed in turnings; but he came to know that he was not doing all these exactly as his master did, so he made some changes, activities and managed to ride the bicycle. In fact he did some manipulations (changes, modifications and did those activities. So perception, imitation and manipulation are the three psychomotor abilities) that we perform when we learn to do some activity. Our psychomotor activities do not stop with mere doing of something. We want to become experts is doing things.

Lalith repeated, practiced it, and made it precise, perfect, and he learnt to pedal precisely well. He gradually stopped doing unnecessary, unrelated movements. After manipulation ability, he learnt the precision ability. But to ride on a cycle he had to do all those activities in co-ordination together, in some order. Otherwise the complex ability of riding on a cycle cannot be learnt. This way of combining co-ordinating, integrating, simple activities to perform a complex activity is know as articulation; he wanted to develop some special ways of doing this, that is, some of his own characteristic way of cycling. Those ways are his own and as he practiced them, they became 'natural' to him. Now he can ride a cycle with ease, without even being, 'conscious' of your cycling activities.

Cycling has become so 'natural with him. This final activity in the psychomotor ability is known as naturalisation. So, to 'learn' a psychomotor skill the abilities required are perception, imitation and manipulation. If you want to manipulation master it, to make it a natural (habitual) way of doing, then you have to learn the precision, manipulation and naturalisation.

Uses of Taxonomy of Education Objectives

1. The taxonomy helps to analyse and classify the objectives.
2. Taxonomy of educational objectives also direct the teacher's as to how the total development of a child be achieved.
3. Taxonomy helps the teacher to identify the behaviour modification and the role of teaching.
4. Taxonomy helps to bring about the relationship between inputs, process and output in teaching, learning and evaluation procedure.
5. The teacher could make use of the knowledge of taxonomy in systematising the teaching-learning process.
6. Helps the teachers and administrators who deal with curricular and evaluation problems to discuss these problems with greater precision.
7. Helps to compare the present goals of education with the past and to identify the additional goals in future, to be included.

8. Objective based curriculum construction could be insisted so that it becomes easy to plan learning experiences and prepare evaluation devices.

9. It is useful to researchers as a frame work for viewing the educational process and analysing its working.

21

Students Evaluating Teachers in Higher Education

Education is the key to unlock the main gate to civilisation and modernisation. It is the most important means to develop individuals and nations and to bring about the desired social reforms in this fast changing world of ours. Education is not only used to bring about constructive and desirable economic, social and political changes but should be an answer to the rising expectations of the people anywhere.

Education is the right to peace, security and better understanding of all mankind. Higher education occupies an important place in the process of nation building. It is a powerful instrument in development. Higher education now is caught between the traditional expectations and the new demands. Young students call for education that helps them relate formal curricula and courses to social needs and search for solutions to societal problems.

In a developing country like India, higher education should have focused goals. India being a secular socialistic republic, it is the duty of the society to provide equal opportunity to all to receive higher education. Higher education sector would need a sustained mechanism to formulate plans for implementing progressive planning. We should also be conscious that higher education system will have to owe an explanation to the society at large for its role in eradication of illiteracy. Formal structural linkages between extension and education are to be made. Special efforts should be taken to adopt latest educational technology and use of mass media by strengthening existing educational media research centres in the country.

Teachers in Higher Education

Traditionally teachers have enjoyed a position of great respect in India. The religious leaders and social reformers have been addressed as teachers. Even today thousands of teachers are still held in esteem by their students and the community. The status and quality of teachers have a direct bearing on the quality education and ultimately on the quality of nation.

A College or University stands or falls by its teachers. Teachers can make or mar the image of a college. The teachers should carry themselves with mobility, dignity and scholarship. Teachers of higher education should be people bent on perfection, bubbling with enthusiasm over ideas. They should read, write and speak great thoughts. They need constant insistence on quality and excellence.

No teacher should say "I can accept my good students, those who behave and do good work, but I cannot accept those who do not work, who have the wrong attitude and who cause me trouble" as acceptance of all these gives power to the teacher. Teaching is a challenging job only when we give fully of ourselves that we can become our best selves.

It is said that quality of the citizens depends on the quality of education and the quality of education in turn depends on the quality of teachers. A teacher teaches the students not only the subject matter but also becomes a moral counselor of those whom he teaches. He is expected to follow the right type of strategies of teaching and evaluation techniques and be an efficient organiser and administrator.

It has been observed that the student's achievement was affected by the following factors: 1. Inadequate information about students and their background, 2. Inappropriate perception of student behaviour, 3. Inadequate monitoring of student behaviour, 4. Authoritative handling of classrooms, 5. Poor handling of classrooms, 6. Poor communication skill, 7. Lack of mastery over the content, 8. Poor moral standard, 9. Inappropriate teaching skill and 10. Bias or partiality.

The teacher should aid a student until he learns. He has to reinforce the learners. Teacher can ignores, punish, pray for, cajole, prescribe, lecture, repeat and mediate to facilitate learning. He should also arrange conditions that are external to the learners to improve their learning.

Teachers should treat their students with love and affection. They must be impartial to all students and help them grow intellectually, physically, socially, emotionally and morally. Teachers should cultivate in students respect for manual work and dignity of labour.

Effective teachers must care passionately both for their subject matter and their students. They must make greater use of effective modes of teaching and train students to take greater responsibility for their learning. This can be achieved through diversification of teaching style. Learning technologies should be designed to increase and not reduce the amount of personal contact between students and faculty on intellectual issues.

Teachers should grow continuously in their academic and professional life, involve themselves in research activities, participate in seminars, workshops, conference, orientation programmes participate in extra and co-curricular activities and accept membership in professional organisations, communities to update their knowledge and skills.

Accountability in Education

Accountability in education refers to the practice of holding educational systems responsible for the quality of their products–students' knowledge, skills, behaviour and attitude. Accountability in education also means that someone, a public or private agent, will be held answerable for performing as agreed upon. After agreement/norms have been reached upon objectives, decisions have to be made about the input to achieve the objectives, measuring instrument could be used to determine the degree to which the objectives have been met. Each member of any organisation is expected to answer someone for doing specific things according to specific plans and against certain time table to accomplish tangible performance results.

Student Evaluating Teacher Performance

The concept of student evaluating teachers has not been properly understood or utilised. Validity, relevance, acceptability, objectivity, need and utility of student evaluation should be clearly understood. Malhotra committee considered three modes of evaluation of teacher performance. Evaluation by students/ex-students, self appraisal by teachers and evaluation by peers and heads of departments/ institutions

Evaluation of teachers' performance could be undertaken on the basis of the following variables, in terms of number of teachers, and students activities involved in teacher performance, type of colleges and institutions, quality of students admitted, library and laboratory facilities available, concept, need, objectives, purpose and utility of student evaluation and in terms of reliability and validity of such evaluation procedure.

Purpose of Student Evaluation

Evaluation of teacher performance helps in three ways: a data base objective assessment of teacher performance will enable the system to have a measure of accountability; an objective assessment of all the activities of a teacher will enable an appraisal of individuals strengths and weaknesses in order that certain remedial action will be suggested for overcoming weaknesses. to evolve, on the basis of this appraisal and evaluation, a set of guidelines for future.

It will also provide a basis for informed administrative decisions and quality teaching will be recognised and rewarded. The social reinforcement of getting favourable ratings will provide added incentive for the improvement of teaching. The feedback from student evaluation is useful to the improvement of teaching.

Purpose

Students are expected to evaluate a series of activities and jobs performed by the teacher in the classroom and outside pertaining to student interactions with the teacher.

This assessment over a period of three years is accumulated and will serve to identify the strengths and weaknesses of the teacher. Strong points can be used to reward the teachers in the form of promotion/career advancement and for best teacher awards.

Competence of Students to Evaluate Teachers

When it is acceptable to the teachers that they could be evaluated by the students, the question arises whether the students have the competence to evaluate the teachers? Whether there should be some discrimination in assigning this responsibility to students? At what level the students are ready to evaluate the teachers' competence-at UG level or at the PG level? Should brilliant students alone evaluate or all the students with whom the teacher interacts? Whether the students who are regular in attending the classes are more competent to evaluate than who are irregular?.

The teachers' task is to teach every one in the class irrespective of their abilities and interest. An effective teacher takes into account the individual differences and caters to their needs and makes them learn better. Hence, it becomes imperative that all the students should be permitted to evaluate the teachers. Teachers should thus have a positive attitude towards students evaluating them.

Criteria for Evaluating Teacher Performance

We should have definite criteria on which the teachers could be evaluated so that the students are clear and definite about what is to be evaluated without any ambiguity.

Criteria on which the teachers to be evaluated are given below which could be used for self appraisal by teachers, evaluation by students and evaluation by peers and heads of departments. The evaluation could be done on a Five Point Scale and consolidated for the total scores.

	Very often	*Often*	*Some-time*	*Rarely*	*Never*
I. Teacher's personality					
1. Pleasing					
2. Rigid					
3. Introvert					
4. Dogmatic					
5. Considerate					
6. Business like					
7. Persistent					
8. Extrovert					
9. Committed					
10. Intelligent					
11. Friendly					
12. Fair					

13. Sincere
14. Unassuming
15. Punctual
16. Sociable
17. Self confidence
18. Authoritarian.

II. Knowledge of students and their background

1. Calling the students by their names
2. Knows the family conditions
3. Easy to approach
4. Identifies the problems of students
5. Helps the students solve the problems
6. Willing to provide guidance
7. Shows interest in the welfare of students
8. Help to modify student behaviour
9. Understands ability and interest of students
10. Organizes tutorial to the students
11. Does not show any bias
12. Tries to promote desirable personality traits in students
13. Supervises students closely
14. Exhibits strong disapproval.

III. Mastery over the subject–Content area

1. Has mastery over the content
2. Upto date in the subject
3. Shows willingness to know more
4. Writes papers/books
5. Participates in seminar/conference/workshop
6. Has good reading habit
7. Shows interest in attending in-service programme
8. Exhibits readiness for learning
9. Shows enthusiasm in presenting new concepts
10. Has aptitude for teaching.

IV. Teaching strategy

1. Prepares well for the class, able to formulate and attain objectives
2. Chooses appropriate teaching techniques
3. Permits interaction in the class
4. Presents content with clarity
5. Good communicator
6. Question the students
7. Employs gestures and facial expressions
8. Holds students' interest throughout the class
9. Uses aids appropriately
10. Encourages students to question

11. Explains well
12. Accepts and encourage students' answers
13. Relates the knowledge to the life
14. Democratic in the class
15. Plans and executes with student
16. Relaxed in the class
17. Uses humour in appropriate place
18. Helps students reduce tension
19. Elicits student participation
20. Starts and finishes on time the class
21. Reinforce with reward
22. Punishes bad behaviour
23. Contacts parents
24. Establishes good human relation
25. Encourages self expression.

V. Evaluation Techniques Employed

1. Employs appropriate technique to evaluate
2. Uses evaluation to identify the difficulties of students
3. Evaluates to find out whether objectives are achieved
4. Uses the result to help the students learning
5. Objective and impartial
6. Prompts in correcting the test/assignment paper

7. Uses the results as a feedback and modify methods of teaching
8. Encourages self-assessment
9. Uses peer group assessment
10. Encourages original and creative answer
11. Gives direction
12. Diagnoses and prepare remedial measure.

VI. Teacher and the extra and Co-curricular activities

1. Participates in all the college activities
2. Takes initiate to organise extra and co-curricular activities
3. Concentrates only on the responsibilities assigned
4. Encourages students taking up responsibilities
5. Encourages students to participate in extra and co-curricular activities
6. Exhibits a positive attitude towards extra and co-curricular activities
7. Enlists the co-operation of other staff in organising programme
8. Encourages the students to develop value system
9. Appreciates students talents.

VII. Teachers' Interaction with others

1. Friendly with colleagues
2. Gets co-operation from all colleagues
3. Co-operates with other staff

4. Adjusts with the head and others
5. Shows positive attitude toward the head and others
6. Helps in toning the institutional climate
7. Sincere and accountable
8. Exhibits high level of professional involvement
9. Observes the code of conduct of teaching profession
10. Hostile towards the head
11. Hostile towards the colleagues
12. Criticizes others.

Scoring will depend on the type of statement given in the criteria whether positive or negative. Total scores will show the teacher' quality to be an effective teacher with the concern for the students, mastery over the subjects taught, teaching and evaluation strategy employed.

22

Linkage between Higher Education and Community–GRI Experience

"True education must correspond to the surrounding circumstances or it is not a healthy growth"

—Mahathma Gandhi

The Education that does not benefit society and the society which does not realise the full potential of education are both futile. Education and Society are the two sides of the same coin and are reciprocally beneficent. The term society refers not to a mere group of people but a complex pattern of the forms of interactions that raise among and between them. Growth and exploitation of new knowledge are the key and deciding factors of the prosperity of any society. Especially in the present circumstances where world is often described as a global village unless one updates his knowledge and strives to realise his full potential survival is neigh impossible. It has become imperative in this competitive world to have a sound system of education that would enable one to achieve the standards of living enjoyed by the developed nation. It is the knowledge gained through education that makes an individual contribute his mite to make a vibrant society. Education rightly labeled as knowledge industry manufactures sound products only in collaboration with user needs, demand driven with community participation.

Paper to be presented in the Seminar Session of the Vice-Chancellors' Conference of ACU, held at Belfast, on 1st, 2nd September, 2003.

The major function of education is to produce socially fit persons who are conversant with the social traditions and cultural background. Only those educational institutions which are equipped to coordinate with community can produce quality people who would work in tune with the social needs and demands reflecting ethos, aims and values of the society, having imbibed them through concerted effort.

The father of our nation Mahatma Gandhi visualised education as an instrument of national development and as a basic tool for the development of consciousness and reconstruction of the society.

GRI in Capsule

The Gandhigram Rural Institute (Deemed University) was founded by Dr. (Mrs.) T.S. Soundaram and Dr. G. Ramachandran, the disciples of the great seer-Mahatma Gandhi, in 1947, with the vision to promote integrated rural development.

Situated in the Southern part of India, adjacent to the famous temple city, Madurai, Gandhigram Rural Institute is dedicated to rural upliftment. Among many experiments in rural development, education was one. Gandhiji's system of education 'Naitalim' was experimented from Pre-School to Higher Education. The Rural Institute was started in 1956 to cater to the needs of rural mass for higher education and attained Deemed University status in 1976 in recognition of its services to the upliftment of the rural mass through education. In 2002, it added an important milestone to its history by being accredited with 5 star status by the National Assessment and Accreditation Council of India.

Ours is an educational institution which strives to make Gandhiji's dream a reality. We believe that education should bring about a transformation and move towards a humane and enlightened society. Our curriculum is based on participatory education, participatory planning and participatory democracy and in the words of Gandhi again "the goal is to establish a non-violent and non-exploiting social and economic order".

GRI and Community

Our curriculum has three dimensions one leading to the other, one intertwined with the other-Teaching, Research and Extension Consumer requirements are taken into consideration and the Curriculum is designed to fulfill the needs and demands of the society. The felt needs of the society are identified through our constant interaction with the community. Our students and the staff interact with people during their visits and village placement programme, and people come to GRI with their needs and the problems. This becomes the basis for our curriculum construction.

Developing knowledge through teaching and research and development through outreach programmes have been the core of GRI. Courses offered in GRI are grouped into three major categories such as Social Sciences, Sciences and Languages. This paper has attempted to bring to light how each discipline is community linked, and socially relevant. A brief scanning surfaces in the following paragraphs the contributions of each subject to the community.

I. Social Sciences

The main objective of the courses offered is to understand the structure of the society, issues, problems of people and to identify suitable strategies to enable the mass to find solution to their problems. It emphasises the life long process of to Be by Learning to Become.

(i) Rural Development and Management is equivalent to management studies of other conventional universities. The main difference is that the focus is on rural development and aim is to train students to become Non-Governmental and Governmental officials equipped to manage issues creatively and realistically.

(ii) Sociology teaches the students to study community from cultural, anthropological, economic, feminist perspective and train the students to tackle social issues and preserve the culture.

(iii) Business Economics focuses on economic development and sustainability, meeting supply-demand and marketing issues. The weekly seminars in which students interact with those in service in various fields and other public sectors enable the students to discriminate between illusions and reality.

(iv) Cooperative Management is a subject which is a pioneering effort of our university to strengthen the cooperative spirit and movements and help to organise cooperative societies and banks which cater to the needs of the community.

(v) Rural Industries and Management an undergraduate course helps to promote appropriate technologies in rural industries. These small-scale industries provide employment to masses.

(vi) Micro level planning is another programme which focuses on planning at the community level, thus making planning need based with the participation of the stockholder. Micro finance, Micro Credit System, Local Governance, Health and Hygiene, which are the essentials of life are thought of, planned and executed. Students are trained for this purpose.

(vii) In Development Administration the students are taught to participate in the organic growth and practices of governance, Panchayati raj Institutes, empowerment of local leaders apart from being taught subjects like politics, history etc. The students actively participate in Youth Parliament Programmes to understand and preserve democracy. They regularly interact with Panchayat officials and get an insight into governance at the grass root.

II. Sciences

The major objective of teaching science in GRI is to enable the students to develop scientific knowledge, aptitude and apply it to help rural mass to have a better life style and the community to enjoy the inventions and discoveries of science and technology.

1. Chemistry taught in our university is different from the conventional course in the sense the subject learnt in the laboratories is taken to the community to tackle social issues such as water pollution due to tanneries and dyeing units, fluoride, corrosion etc. Many such problems are solved by the students and staff of the Department.

2. Department of Physics helps the community in the use and maintenance of simple electrical and electronic apparatus. Through Lab-to-Land programmes the students of this discipline take science and technology to villages by developing science kit to teach in schools.

3. Department of Biology offers courses on medicinal plants, mushroom cultivation and agro products. The department trains rural youth, especially women, in mushroom cultivation and weekly interaction between the students and nearby village community is part of the curriculum.

4. Home Science department apart from offering subjects like food and nutrition, textile and clothing, child development and care, home management, organises periodic camps in the community with active participation of the students on different issues relating to above. The department runs a day care centre for local community as well as for the benefit of children from neighbouring villages.

5. Agriculture faculty and Krishi Vigyan Kendra (KVK) reach out to the community and spread the new technologies in farming, cattle and poultry rearing and dairy products. They have created the awareness and its input could be seen at least in 100 villages.

6. Sanitation Faculty trains students to become Sanitary Inspectors. It has adopted nearby villages where better and total sanitary facilities are provided with the help of the students and the community. The total sanitation project has made the women folk realise the use of toilets and to demand for toilets in their community.

7. Rural Technology is a novel programme offered by our university where students are trained in production of cost effective materials and construction and food preservation techniques. The motto of this department is "House for all" which is possible through their innovative low cost building construction programmes.

8. Computer Science Programme not only trains students in computer application and information technology but also it takes it to nearby villages. The neighbouring villages are provided with computers and linked to our university. The people, farmers, women and children of neighbouring community get the benefit of information technology at their door steps.

III. Languages

Languages are effective vehicles for communication. We have two faculties at present. One is English and Foreign Languages and the other is Tamil and Indian Languages.

1. English faculty runs a course called English and Communication studies. which help students to communicate the information to the community as journalists and media persons. This department helps to promote teaching English in schools. Teachers from schools are trained to use various techniques.

2. Tamil faculty apart from teaching Tamil Literature concentrates on training the students in folk arts. The students get first hand knowledge of the varied folk arts in India, especially in Tamil Nadu by visiting and collecting information from the community. Traditional arts and culture found in the community are revived through our interaction with the people.

One might wonder how this close linkage with the community has become possible and where one finds the time for interaction with the community. One may even suspect that the syllabus is so dilute that much of the time is spent on community interaction. Curriculum in GRI is heavy and standardised as that of any other university. We have one unique feature that makes close communication with neighbouring communities possible which is our outreach programme which is explained in the next section.

IV. Outreach Programme

The University at the Village Doorstep has been one of our innovative programmes with the following objectives:

- To enrich the learning process of students and faculty through exposure to community needs, problems and issues;

- To impart training in development-oriented activities to grassroots development workers, officials and non-officials drawn from NGOs, government departments, banks, training and research organisations;
- To organise knowledge and skill-based training for a wide-spectrum of clients from local institutions such as Panchayats, cooperatives and other community-based formal and informal organisations;
- To undertake socially relevant action-oriented research and analysis for the betterment of the rural community; and
- To bring out changes in the living conditions of different sections of the rural community.

Every student is expected to spend a minimum period of 4 days every semester under Village Placement Programme apart from regular and periodic visits to the villages. Every department adopts a village for its intensive programme. They stay amidst the villagers, observing their living pattern, working schedule, analysing their problems and through participatory appraisal help them to reach at some solution. This has motivated students to commit themselves to services of the community.

V. Research

Academic profundity combines with practical wisdom in the Research programmes. Most of our research programmes are undertaken with thrust on community development and on rural upliftment. There are Fellows working in Rural Development, Sociology, Home Science, Economics, Agriculture to promote rural industries, empowerment of women; ranging from leadership qualities in Panchayati leaders to feminism in literary works of various countries; starting from micro level planning at grassroot level and going up to studying profitable trade and marketing of goods.

It is not an exaggeration to say the three pronged approach has made the GRI Experience an enriched one.

Apart from these courses we have two centres exclusively devoted to rural upliftment. The Adult and Population Education Centre is dedicated to bringing about total literacy. Intensive drive to make every one literate has been taken by our Adult Continuing Education department. Rural Libraries are established to continue their education. To help our students aware of the population production in the country PERC undertakes training the staff and students in other schools and colleges.

The Renewable Energy Centre has been concentrating on finding alternative energy sources such as Solar, Wind energy through researches and training the village youths to install and maintain the equipment.

Theoretical knowledge is always linked with practical implementation lending credibility to all our programme.

VI. Co-Curricular Activities

The Co-curricular activities of our institute is also oriented towards community. In the place of N.C.C. we have Shanthi Sena. The Warriors of peace are trained to wage war with violence and disharmony. Whenever there are communal riots, natural calamities our Shanthi Sainiks and N. S. S. Volunteers stand first among equals. The Physical Education Department, apart from building the physique of our students train the village community in various sports activities. The education provided at GRI strives for a wholesome and all round growth of our own students and also those in our locale.

Conclusion

Education, in order to be effective should be techno-informative, provide opportunities to acquire skills by engaging students in a variety of processes and situations and above all provide a climate for the nature of values both as a personalised set of values forming one's character and including necessarily social, cultural and national values so as to have a context and meaning for action and decision. Education must play an interventionist as well as catalystic role for promoting national cohesion and empowering the students not only to meet personal challenges but also to become agents of social change. The Gandhigram Rural Institute's experience in the field of education, research and extension has so far been enriching and rewarding. This university with a national character, we hope and pray, will soon find a prominent place in the world map as a university committed to the Community.

23

Linkage between Universities and Communities Action Programmes

Why Linkages

Educational Institutions should become integral part of the community in which they are located and take the best from the environment in which they exist. Necessarily they need to give the best to the society. Mere imparting of academic knowledge should not be the sole aim of educational institutions. They should go beyond this and imbibe the spirit of 'concern for the community' and social accountability among the students which in turn would help them establish link with various sections of the community. Institutes of higher education have expertise in various disciplines. Their knowledge should be fully utilised for the betterment of the community.

There should be a frequent interaction between the universities and communities for which the following action programmes are suggested:

1. University Department wise/College wise liaison Officer or Coordinator for the community could be created so as to activate the community linkages.

2. University Volunteers scheme (UVS) by involving NSS passed out students may be instructed to work for the betterment of the community.

3. Village Level Volunteers Bank (VLVB) may be created to establish link between the university and community.

4. Universities may create District level Forum (DLF) in which all the government department officials and the village panchayat leaders/key village leaders under the traditional setting could gather and discuss at length the pressing problems in the community.

5. University department 'on wheels (or) the concept of Mobile University' may be introduced for the benefit of the village communities for the people who cannot otherwise have the opportunity for higher education.

6. Community college/community polytechnic under the university system could deliver benefits to the community.

7. On-the-spot problem solving sessions may be conducted in villages with the help of Government officials as well as with faculties in the university.

8. Constant and consistent touch with community for which university/college may use 'village as a living classroom.'

9. Every university may organise 'Grievance Day' so as to hear the problems of the community, undertake an analysis and represent the matter to the concerned district.

10. Block level Technology Centres may be established to provide technical support to the needy in the community.

Appropriate technology in construction work could be imparted through this centre. New technologies like water harvesting, smokeless chulas, developing drudgery free equipment, etc., could be promoted. High technologies like Information technology, Computer could be taken to the communities for their effective use.

- A periodical inter-religious prayer/dialogue/ community prayer involving all the leaders may be organised at the village, block and district level to inculcate value system.

- Every temple/church/mosque in the community may be used as 'Divine Realisation Centre' (DRC) or Self-realisation Centre.

- University cum Rural Growth Network Village Thinkers Forum (UVTF) or University cum NGO Thinkers Forum may be created to think about the plight of the village communities.

- University Volunteers Bank (UVB) may be created so as to enroll volunteers from the community besides NSS to promote voluntarism and to serve the community

- 'Gandhi Ghar'-'Gandhi Hut' may be created in villages to inculcate Gandhian values.

- Community Based University Hostels (CBUH) may be started which will provide opportunity to students to understand the realities of the community.

- Community shops may be established with a view to serve them and to ensure people's participation. Community shops being the general provisions store will gradually stop exploitation.

- Village folk arts/songs may be encouraged and efforts may be taken to organise periodical cultural programmes with a view to generate awareness in the community.

- Micro Level Data Bank (MLDB) may be maintained in the university with the help of the village panchayats and prepare a profile for each village.
- Organise training programmes in small trades, farming for capacity building to the youths and farmers.
- Each university may develop a 'Model Village' for the holistic development of the community.
- Every individual department in the university may be encouraged to give their own plan for community development/neighbourhood outreach programme.
- Career guidance and counseling centres in the heart of the community will create confidence among the parents of budding youth.
- Creation of children's club, youth club, women's club (self help groups), farmers' club and association of the aged or day care centre for the aged will keep lively contacts between the university and community.
- A novel idea 'Weekly Night Stay in Villages' (WNSV) may be carried out through university departments. It is a successful experiment of IDARA, Gandhigram since the last quarter of 1999.
- Necessary efforts may be taken to organise FOYOM–Fortnight Youth Meet and monthly women's mela in the neighbourhood/community so as to analyse the problems of youth and women to find solutions.
- Week end school/Evening school for youth in peace and nonviolence may be introduced in order to attack violence.

- *Community based 'Shramdhan' activities may be promoted. Village/Block/District level Shramdhan can create the concept of clean environment. Neighbouring city cleaning campaign will attract the urban dwellers.

- A small percentage of university library budget may be allocated to set up Rural Libraries in the community. Otherwise, 'Mobile Library' may be maintained for the enrichment of communities.

- Taking University to the door steps of village' has been experimented by GRI and it may be replicated.

- Village Placement Programme (VPP) could be thought of which is a successful experiment in Gandhigram.

- Health for All and environmental sanitation campaign could be organised.

- Village Planning Committees (VPC) or Micro level Planning Committees (MPC) may be thought of with the assistance of universities.

- Youth Peace Brigade (YPB) may be created in all the villages to bring peace to the community.

- Attractive 'Wall Posters' on important issues could be prepared and displayed by universities periodically.

- All the 29 subjects mentioned in the schedule of New Panchayati Raj System and the role of higher education institutions may be dealt with by different departments.

- Science clubs/Eco clubs/Science for villages may be started in every school and the village community to spread the science concepts.

- Drug de-addiction centers/Free legal service for poor/Baby care centre/Balwadis in all the villages of each university area may be started.
- Service to orphans/destitute/aged may be rendered.
- Welfare and rehabilitation programmes for Disabled may be streamlined in the community.
- A network of NGO's/Individual Social Workers/ Volunteers meet may be organised periodically.
- Public Distribution System (PDS) may be regulated with the assistance of students.
- Youth Leadership Training Programme (YLTP) may be conducted periodically for the benefit of youth.
- Village Priest Association (VPA) may be organised so as to involve the priests in the development process.
- Individual/Family Tension Releasing Centre (FTRC) in the village community may be created like family counseling.
- Community Sanitation Movement may be launched either under the banner of NSS or under the umbrella of university.
- Information Board and 'Thought for the Day' may be displayed in the prominent places of the community under the guidance of university.
- Important monuments could be identified and protected by Universities/Departments/Colleges.
- Vital village centres like village schools, village panchayats, village cooperatives, village assembly, village temples and village leaders are to be directly linked with faculties/departments.

- Traditional scholars/pundits in the village setting may be encouraged and their creative writings could be utilised.
- Village festivals may be used as an occasion where University could think of providing some inputs to the community by organising exhibitions, demonstrations etc.
- Universities could play a vital role to eradicate superstitious believes in the village community with scientific explanations.
- Social evils like dowry, child labour, female infanticide and other problems may be uprooted through constant interaction.
- Efforts may be taken to work for peace and communal harmony through inter-religious prayers in the community.
- *Village conflicts may be prevented and resolved by the universities without police and court. Village court may created by universities with service minded legal experts. Universities may take efforts to prevent road accidents with the help of transport crew/officials.
- University Blood Bank (UBB) could serve the local community
- Geography and history of the local community may be made available with the university so as to educate the youth.
- The local issues/problems/crises at all levels may be highlighted in mass media for which universities could play a vital role.
- Universities may honour the local leaders highlighting their contributions.

- Universities may work for zero violence, zero dowry, zero pollution, zero garbage, zero untouchability, zero alcohol/drugs, zero poverty, zero unemployment, zero conflict, zero exploitation, zero crime, zero divorce etc. with a view to create sarvodaya society/community.

In conclusion, it may be said that every university/higher education Institute can serve as a light house of the community.

Modus Operandi

- Each university/college can choose a panchayat and may propose to work in that panchayat for a period of five years.
- To begin with, an extensive study using participatory methods may be undertaken to find out the socio-economic status and problems of the community. Their needs and aspirations may be assessed through such study.
- The findings of the study may be shared with the community and an action plan to solve the problems and also to fulfill the needs of the community may be prepared with the active participation of the community.
- The action plan may include the problems-the solutions to each problem-the agreed solution-activities proposed-implementation strategy-roles and responsibilities of stakeholders and the–university/colleges
- Time frame for completing the activity
    - financial requirement
    - contribution from people/people participation

- monitoring and evaluation indicators
- expected outcome

A Committee consisting of President and Ward-members Panchayat, representatives from Self-Help Groups (SHGs) and; other formal and informal groups, informal leaders, NGOs, ~ student representatives and faculty representative may be constituted to implement and monitor the programme.

Merits of Linkages

Linkages with the community is mutually beneficial. The merits are many. Prominent among them are.

- students and staff are exposed to the realities of life outside the portals of educational institutions;
- get trained in micro-level planning;
- students and staff tend to develop the spirit of "Concern for the Community";
- helps build up a good and long-lasting relationship between the college/university and the community;
- community may also contribute for the development of the college/university in course of time;
- provide excellent scope for doing action-oriented research in rural areas;
- helps in creating a harmonious atmosphere in the community;
- facilitates overall holistic development of the community;
- facilitates in developing effective linkages among different agencies working for rural development;

- helps in optimal use of resources available both in universities/colleges and community;
- builds up the capacity of the people and ultimately may end up in self-mobilisation.

Risks and Uncertainties in Establishing Linkages

- Lack of positive attitude on the part of the students and faculty and other government agencies;
- Paucity of required expertise in the universities/ colleges;
- Want of required funds to initiate and sustain the linkages;
- Time constraints for staff and students;
- Want of required support from government institutions;
- Existence of factions and feuds in the village;
- Vested interests of participating organisations.

24

Renewable Energy Development: The Need of the Hour

Introduction

Energy is the primary resource and essential for all development, so much so that per capita consumption of energy has come to be taken as an index of development of a nation. Choice of source of energy indicates the civilisation of mankind. Inventions of different types of fuels and use of these in technologies play a crucial role in the development of a nation whereas the energy and technology sources which we use today are not ecologically and environmentally conducive. They are depleting every day. At work, at play, in the home, school or in the street, field, factory or office, in a village or a city, all living creatures–young and old, small or large and even non-living machines need and use energy in some form or the other. Energy plays a vital role in the economic development of a nation, because, it helps in cultivation of crops, helps us to cook food, keeps people alive, keeps our houses warm or cool, runs industries, transports goods and people, fuels economic development and sustains economic systems and progress. Economic growth, social mobility and cultural expression are unthinkable without energy. Energy is thus, the very basis, from the ancient days to till date, and without energy, there would be no life. What type of energy would encourage this? Have we ever thought of for the survival of life on the Planet?

Renewable Energy Development: Why?

The energy crisis of 1973, 1979 and 1991 reminded the world that a country's economy is intimately linked to its energy supplies and prompted almost every country to take stock of its potential supply and demand and to take a serious look at measures to conserve and exploit alternative energy sources without exhausting the present sources of energy like Coal, mineral and oils. Energy supply has been a dominant concern of both the developed and the developing countries of the world in the past several decades. It may be observed from the World Development Report 2001-2002, the per capita consumption of energy in India was about 6.0 per cent of that in Canada, 5.9 per cent in the United States, 8. 7 per cent in Norway and 11. 7 per cent in Japan. This clearly shows the fact that India has the second largest population (1030 million) and one of the lowest per capita income ($450) and the lowest per capita consumption of energy (479 kilogram of oil equivalent). In order to increase the per capita energy consumption, it is the responsibility of the planners and scientists to explore the possibility of producing more quantity of energy, especially energy from renewable sources, which will at the same time, reduce the environmental pollution. We should opt for non-conventional energy sources like solar, wind, biomass, geothermal heat etc. These sources are eco-friendly and free from environmental pollution.

Our country is aimed to achieve 8 per cent growth rate in the economy, then it would commensurate inputs of different energy sources; most of these will be in the form of fossil fuels (coal, oil, natural gas) and electricity. In order to achieve the growth rate prescribed by the planners, there is a need to supply uninterrupted (power) energy to different economic sectors of the Indian economy. Hence renewable energy development must be given priority in the years to come.

The electrical power capacity in the country has increased from 1300MW at the time of independence to about 102,000MW as of December 2001–a near 1000 fold increase over a period of 50 years. Of this, about 70 per cent comes from coal, gas and oil based generation, while about 25 per cent comes from hydro-electricity. Of the balance 5 per cent, about 3 per cent comes from renewable energy sources, while only 2 per cent is generated from nuclear sources. It clearly indicates a fact that our energy production as well as energy consumption is not environment friendly. Hence there is need for the development of renewable energy sources, which are eco-friendly in nature.

Presently the oil import bill stands at 32.0 per cent of the total domestic exports. Imports of crude petroleum products have increased steeply from $6. 4 billion in 1998-99 to $15. 6 billion in 2000-01 (Economic Survey 2001-2002). Further, the domestic oil production and consumption indicate that domestic oil reserves can be exhausted in another 25 years of time. Mineral economists feel that coal will be available for another 215 years. Consumption of oil and coal can damage the environment. In order to avoid environmental pollution, we have to develop and promote, alternative renewable energy sources, which will not pollute the environment.

Over 85 per cent of villages in a country are officially electrified but most villages have less than 20 per cent households actually having electricity connections. There are about 80000 villages in the country which are still to be electrified. Of these, there are an estimated 18000 villages located in remote and difficult areas which cannot be electrified by conventional grid extension. Most of the villages are on hills, forest, deserts and islands. These villages are to be electrified through decentralised power generation using non-conventional sources such as solar, biomass, and small hydropower.

Our expanding economy and the strong growth, expects in the first few decades of the new century, will require additional energy. The use of fossil fuel is likely to dominate our energy strategy in the near and medium term. However, our own resources are finite, and will be available for a limited period. With steady increasing prices, fossil fuel use is also linked to environmental problems particularly global warming, acid rain and other changes in the climate. The challenges of the present energy scene offer us an opportunity to think of alternative renewable energy sources to reduce the dependence of fossil fuel by expanding and diversifying our energy supply mix and shifting the development path towards sustainability as well as environmental and social responsibility.

The oil crises, urbanisation, modernisation, industrialisation, commercialisation, consumerisation and the worldwide exhaustion of hydro carbon fuel (oil and natural gas) in the near future have led all concerned nations, including India, to search for alternative, preferably renewable and sustainable, pollution free sources of energy.

Strategies for Renewable Energy Development

Our country has some special features of energy demand and energy supply, which requires special strategies. If we look at the energy data, the demand for energy is greater than the supply of energy and therefore creates the 'energy gap'. This may lead to 'energy crisis' in future. This gap can be filled in, by adopting appropriate energy demand management (closing down all petrol bunks on holidays, odd and even number vehicles can be allowed to run on road on alternative days, energy education, environmental education etc.) and supply management strategies (exploitation of renewable energy sources, R&D on renewable energy etc.) While adopting these strategies, it is important to look at energy along with other dimensions such as environment, ecology, economics and equity. Furthermore, the strategies for solving energy problems should include technology and management, renewable and non-renewable energy sources, energy conservation, centralised and decentralised energy systems etc.

In a country like India, where the central power system is unreliable and unable to penetrate deep into the villages, the only option appears to be promoting decentralised energy programmes with renewable sources. India being basically an agriculture country with share of about 30 per cent contribution to GDP (1996), the continued non-availability of energy to rural area is bound to impede rural development and progress. One should not fail to take note of the fact that about 70 per cent of population lives in rural areas and any neglect will lead to lopsided growth leading to large migration of population from rural to urban areas which could result in the breakdown of urban infrastructure that is already under great stress.

The Working Group on Power constituted by Planning Commission to formulate the 10th Five Year Plan has estimated a feasible capacity addition of 47,000 MW during the 10th Plan. This plan also emphasizes the need to ensure enhancement of the quality of life. In the area of energy, this principle can be translated to mean "Energy for all"; to meet the cooking and lighting needs of the people. It is against this backdrop, the renewable energy strategy for the 10th plan period has been formulated, keeping in view the overall renewable energy policy perspective for the medium term of 2000-2012, which covers the 10th and 11th Plan periods. The Renewable Energy Plan 2012 sets medium-term targets to be achieved until 2012. These are:

- Deployment of solar water heating systems in one million homes
- Electrification by renewable energy source of at least one quarter of 18,000 un-electrified villages
- Deployment of five million solar lanterns and two million solar home lighting systems
- Coverage of 30 million households through improved chulhas and
- Setting up of a further three million family sized biogas plants.

An Overview of Renewable Energy Technologies

The possible renewable and non-conventional energy sources are solar, wind, tidal, wave, geothermal, Ocean Thermal Energy, biomass, biogas, Bagasse based plants etc. These renewable sources have great potential and available in plenty in our country, but has not been exploited fully. Unless we tap these resources for our requirements the earth will get destroyed soon.

Significance of Renewable Non Conventional Energy Sources

- Unlimited–available in Plenty
- Perennial source
- Environment friendly–No emission of polluting gases which cause greenhouse effect and acid rains
- Favoured options for sustainable development
- naturally recycled resource base
- Decentralised energy option–energy generation is centralised
- Cost effective use of local resources which are available both in rural and urban areas.
- Easy to install and operate
- Offers opportunity for rural electrification
- Generates rural employment–by capacity building to manufacture and maintain the devices
- Fuel transportation costs eliminated when generated and used locally
- Safe operation without environmental hazards.

Conclusion

Located in the tropical region, India is endowed with abundant natural resources. For all resources, directly or indirectly, sun is a source for all energy on the earth. Solar energy radiation is directly received by the earth's surface, and it is constantly creating or manifesting itself in several other forms of renewable energy such as wind, hydro-power, including tidal and wave energy, ocean thermal energy, bio-energy. The solar energy resource-base that naturally recycles or replenishes 'renewable' sources of energy has to be utilised to meet the energy needs of the growing population, projected to be 10 billions by 2050, of whom 2 billion are estimated to be in India.

The multi-prolonged strategies initiated after establishment of Ministry of Non Conventional Energy Sources (MNES) have produced desired results in the area of renewable energy sources. Further, the introduction of 'Urjagram', (Energy village), Integrated Rural Energy Planning, National Project on Biogas Plants and establishment of various state level nodal agencies are yet another contribution made by the MNES. India needs to develop a host of human resources. People with technical know-how should be trained to make the devices function properly in villages. Scientific Institutions and energy scientists should take efforts to reduce the cost of production of renewable energy devices. Further more, social awareness should be created to accept of the renewable energy technologies that promote Sustainable Development which is in harmony with nature and permits future generation to enjoy a standard of living not inferior to what we enjoy today. It also involves responsible stewardship of our earth resources and promotes equity between generations. Mahatma Gandhi has suggested three measures to reduce the consumption of resources in general, and energy resources, in particular. The three are:

1. Changing the life style,
2. Adopting voluntary simplicity, and
3. Reduce, reuse and recycle resources.

Mahatma Gandhi further said, "Nature produces enough to meet the needs of all the people, but not enough to satisfy the greed of any one".

Today's World depends on renewable energy to make this plant livable and have sustainability. We need New World order, based on Renewable Energy Technologies to safeguard this 'Mother Earth'.

25

Environmental Issues and Challenges: Role of Higher Education

We seem to exist in a hazardous time,

Drifting along here through space;

Nobody knows just when we'd begun,

Or how far we've gone in the race.

—Ben King

There was a time when man worshipped Nature and lived amidst it enjoying the serenity that surrounded him. It is hard to say when man began slowly to draw away from Nature allured by the glittering materialistic world. It is hard to say exactly when materialism took over and man began to crave the comforts of prosperity. It is hard to say when the rapid growth of industrialisation resulted in modernisation, slowly destroying the fruits of nature. The modern world is so busy when men "hurry, flurry, scurry and worry" and find no time to "stand and stare" at nature which was once upon a time considered to be the best teacher. Too much of exploitation of Mother Earth has resulted in confused priorities and need for conservation of environment has been pushed far back. There are many causes for the deterioration in environmental preservation.

Causes of Environmental Degradation

In the concern for growth and development man has neglected the very vital aspect that real development is a systematic, methodic, planned affair and any deviation results in hazards. Unplanned development is the first reason for failure in environmental conservation. The rapid rate in which industrialisation is growing causes concern in the minds of human beings as the resultant effects slowly causes eat way environmental purity. Unprecedented growth in modernisation has resulted in excess use of transport which resulted in emission of fuel fumes that pollute air. The need for excess water and unheeded utilisation of water disregarding the factor that water is the elixir of life has borough upon us water scarcity. The necessity to fell down tress to build industries, the explosion in population which has necessitated accommodation facilities and bought down standards of living cause concern and need to be profoundly analysed. Rampant violence and terrorism and the fear of war have urged nation to invent new weapons and strengthen the armaments. Invention and use of missiles and other weapons have polluted environment and caused global warming. This is a serious hazard and if immediate steps are not taken there is a chance of the annihilation of mankind.

Global Concern–Historical Perspective

Realising mankind is on the edge of disaster leaders of nations met and pondered over current situation and means for overcoming the danger of destruction. The UN Conference on Human Environment that met in Stockholm in June 1972 expressed its concern over the danger to the quality of human life and the life in future. Discussions were held on the causes for the continuous degradation of ecological assets. Means of curtailing pollution due to industrial effluents formed part of the discussions. The developing countries were more concerned with poverty alleviation programmes and as they were seeking the fruits of industrialisation pollution was not a major issue for them.

The Stockholm Conference established "United Nations Environment Programme (UNEP) to take measures against environmental pollution and measures for environmental protection. The task of World Commission on "Environment and Development" also known as 'Brundtland Commission' set up in 1983 published its report in 1987 entitled "Our Common Future". The report reiterated "if we continue to use up natural resources as we do at present, if we ignore the plight of the poor, then we can (only) expect a decline in the quality of life". It recommended sustained development at national and international levels.

The World Bank reports of 1992 on 'World Development' and 'Development and environment' sowed the seeds of the World Summit in 1992 at Rio de Janeiro in Brazil. All these efforts resulted in creating awareness among people to face the environmental challenges.

Environmental Challenges

(a) Environmental degradation stands foremost in the list of environmental challenges. The degradation is caused by various factors such as population explosion, unproportionate consumption of available resources, rapid growth in industrialisation and urbanisation, in discriminate and improper use of land which results in soil erosion and makes the land unfit for farming, polluted water and air. Accumulation of bio as well as non-bio degradable waste. These pose grave problems to environmental preservation.

(b) ***Environmental Hazards:*** Most of the natural calamities come under this category. Unexpected landslides, forest fires, earth quakes, eruption of volcano's and floods cause damage not only to human lives but also to the whole earth.

(c) ***Environmental Pollution:*** Effluents from industry, fuel emission, noisy public meetings pose challenges to the environment.

(d) ***Environmental Management:*** Industrial growth, modernisation, urbanisation are inevitable parts of human life at the present world. At the same time, prioritising needs and planning developmental programmes systematically are felt needs.

(e) ***Human Responses:*** "The world has enough for every one's need but not for every one's greed"– Gandhiji. God created this world with all its beauty for the enjoyment of mankind. How man makes use of this rare gift is to be pondered upon. One should realise mindless pursuit of natural prosperity is not the way to happiness. Wealth is not everything and cannot buy everything. Avarice will kill the goose that lays the golden egg. One should realise GNP is not synonymous to better quality of life. Man has to realise absolutely that human existence is part of the eco system and survival depends on eco-balance. At present "little we see in Nature that is outs". We have to have "sustainable development" as suggested by Gandhiji. We should realise that nature should be exploited, but natural resources are renewable. The world in general and India in particular has a rich cultural heritage as well as ecological boons. It is high time we realise that "getting and spending, we lay waste our powers". We Indians have national boundaries, perennial rivers and high mountain ranges. Prudent utilisation of national resources would definitely better the quality of our life. Through proper education necessary wisdom would be developed.

Role of Higher Education Institutions

Education is not mere knowledge gained from text books. Education is a life experience. The higher education institutions with their intellectual expertise should create awareness among people the necessity to preserve environment. They can generate necessary action plan for sustainable development through researches. With uncompromising commitment to principles and practice to protect the planet they can help people to realise the physical, ecological and social dangers encountered by the earth. Awareness on the ethical obligation of the people towards natural resources should be created which would in turn prevent alignment of natural resources. Environmental technologies to preserve the earth should be promoted. The institutions should provide adequate information and guidance to administrators as well as general public on environmental issues and challenges.

Three Dimensional Approach

(a) Teaching should not stop with giving information and facts on particular subject alone, it should incorporate environmental issues in curriculum at all in every subject. Special courses can be organised at undergraduate and post graduate levels such as B.Sc., M.Sc., B.Tech., M.Tech., B.E. and M.E. on environmental science and protection. In addition, we could offer certificate courses for the students and public on environmental issues. As part of co-curricular activities Eco Clubs could be started in every college and university. Watershed management, farming, hill area, and coastal zone development and management should form part of all courses, so that students could take interest in preserving the environment.

(b) ***Research:*** Any research programme becomes meaningful only when it promotes human development and welfare. Interdisciplinary approach to research in Environmental issues at M.Phil. and Ph.D. level should be encouraged. Research projects undertaken on preservation of environment will be an achievement and contribution to the study of environment. Innovative researches in promoting eco friendly industries, machinery and technology, renewable energy sources will promote human welfare and hence should be taken up. A data bank could be compiled by evey institution of higher education to provide necessary information on environmental issues.

(c) ***Extension:*** Extension programmes should focus on creating awareness among people on environmental issues. The students should be encouraged and trained to organise cultural programmes in villages and cities to promote eco-awareness. The governmental and non-governmental agencies should be involved in protecting nature through programmes on rain water harvesting, a forestation, water conservation and environmental protection. Framers should be educated and inspired to go for eco friendly cultivation methods without affecting the nature and industrialists should be motivated towards starting small scale industries to avoid pollution, thus paving a pollution free world.

Conclusion

"We may utilise the gifts of nature just as we choose but in her books the debits are always equal to the credits".

These words of Gandhiji succinctly express the necessity for eco balance. With the abundance of natural gifts man could have attained a serene as well as reasonably prosperous life. In his greed for materials we forgot that the laws of Nature are changeless, unchangeable and there are miracles in the sense of infringement of interruption of Nature's Laws. Behind the magnificent and Kaleidoscopic variety, one discovers in nature a unity of purpose, design and form and if man realises this he can create an eco friendly environment and see an Earthly paradise.

26

Institutes of Higher Education-Instrument for a New Social Order

Education is a lifelong process of growth and activity which brings about changes in the social environment. The process of development is also said to a change for the betterment of human society.

The purpose of universities is not to train the people for specific employment roles but to train them to cope with their lives over the next 50 years, of which job is only one part. The graduates and the Post graduates from universities should try not to be job seekers but be job providers. As Amartya Sen, the Nobel Laureate says, "education is an important tool to bring about socio-economic transformation of any society".

Higher Education is a growth industry and is diversifying at terrific speed.

The 'mental distance' between Academic and Vocational should be removed and it should not be perpetuated.

The Universities in the 21st Century, more than at any time have a responsibility to address the concerns and challenges that are faced by society and to communicate the message that they are indispensable to the knowledge economy.

This could be done by keeping open the doors of university to the Public. Programmes between local schools, students visiting and participating in university activities, involving parents, demonstration in schools, provide expertise services.

University leaders must understand the external impressions of their university, what does public think of us, what we do and how can this be turned to an advantage for initiating engagement.

Any institute of higher education is called excellent only when it involves in community relationship, community development, community empowerment and brings about educational change–thus making education an instrument for social change and brings a new social order. This concept of civic and social responsibilities should be instilled inward to the faculty and outward to the community by the Government, Private Sectors and other stakeholders. A linkage between the University campuses and these agencies are to be promoted to produce active citizens of next generation with social commitment. Links could be established between academic study and services to community through out-reach programmes and by helping the students understand the reality of life and their responsibility and accountability to the society. Faculty should also be given recognition for their service to humanity while giving scholarships and promotions. They should be made to feel that their contributions to the rural development and extension have professional reward and that the investment of their time and energy to the welfare of the people has a payback effect.

The institution should identify and elevate the connection with the stakeholders, the faculty, the students and the community. This organic link will promote social consciousness and responsibility to society as part of social system. A strategic imperative of the institute to this effect will ensure the compliance, capacity and the credibility to take up this extension programme with a mission and objectives.

Man's achievements in the fields of Science and Technology have helped to improve the material conditions of living. Education should develop not only one's intelligence and skills, but also should help to broaden one's outlook and make them useful to society.

In the developing countries like India a large population nearly 75 per cent live in villages. The living standard of these villages is far behind that of urban areas, as the national income of these developing countries is much less than the developed countries. There is imbalance in our investments for rural areas. The standard of living of the people in villages improves only by better use of the physical and human resources as well as service and technology. We could say that we have achieved Gramswaraj. Better and optimum provision for Health and Sanitation, Rural Water Supply, use of energy, communication and information technology and sustainable farming will bring about a total change and development in rural areas.

Development of villages is a crucial issue today. As Gandhi said "the blood of the villages is the cement with which the edifice of the city is built. I want this blood that is today inflating the arteries of the cities to run once again in the blood vessels of the villages". (*Harijan*, 23rd April 1946–p. 198). It is not only that the villages are exploited; the urban dwellers are alienated from the villages. There should be a built in mechanism by which the cosmic unity should be restored by making both rural and urban dwellers come together, and work for the welfare of each other. By analysing the environments of both the cities and villages a via media is to be worked out. There should be a rediscovery of the roots of our culture, traditions and ethos which are embedded in the life of the people in the villages. There should be no poverty either economic or intellectual, in the society. The man exploiting the man or haves' exploiting the have-nots should vanish to restore the peace in the world. The country should move towards planning and executing programmes to raise the standard of living and quality of life of the masses, through education.

An Integrated Approach to Sustainable Rural Development

Rural Development comprises of total/complete development of the villages–both economic and non-economic factors like political, social, health and education. The development in all these dimensions should be sustainable. We should make the villages advance, furthers, evolve and expand by providing needed inputs. This process of societal transformation may be from traditional and conventional to modern or progressive leading to a change in the structure and functions of the society of human dignity, equality and social justice at the grassroots. This approach will take us to an integrated sustainable development. This is possible only where we follow a participatory democratic method. It is a method of governing by the people in real sense, not merely casting their votes. As Mahatma Gandhi said "Gaum gaum me Janata Sarkar and Nagar, nagar me Janata Sarkar" should be established. It should be really the people's Government, Self rule which will lead to "Gram Swaraj". Gram Swaraj will pave the way to economic equality and political freedom will help to achieve decentralised political power to villages. This instills greatest power discipline and responsibility on every individual.

The villages should be self supportive which implies that there should be employment for all to earn their livelihood, land for producing adequate food, crafts for producing clothing and other requirements, shelter for all, institutions for education, health and recreation. All these are governed by the people themselves. If any village develops these facilities without depending upon others, it will lead to: "Gram Swaraj". People will be self reliant with self-confidence and self-respect. The people are to be empowered for this. Education could play a vital role in empowering and equipping the people for creating villages with total development and lead to Gramswaraj.

Curricular Linkages for Rural Development

The universities concentrate on teaching the traditional course like Languages, Humanities, Social Sciences, Sciences, Technology and Medicine. To promote rural development activities, there should be diversification from these conventional courses of study. These courses should be revised to suit the society's requirement for human resources. We need human resources for antipoverty programme, social upliftment, to have good governance, to preserve and cultivate the cultural ethos of our country, to promote self-confidence and to be responsible citizens of the country. There is need for technically trained and qualified personnel for rural development programme. Researches should also be need based, development oriented and result oriented encompassing the objective of integrated sustainable rural development leading to Gramswaraj. What is learnt in the class rooms and researched should be taken to the villages through the out-reach programme–extension the third dimension.

Anti-Poverty Programme

An innovative curriculum should be attempted to prepare the human resources needed in the field of economic growth of this country. It is not merely the theories and principles of economic that will satisfy the requirement. Programmes that will promote the economic status of the individual and the nation should be thought of. Courses like, Agriculture, Small scale industries, Appropriate Technology, Energy Resource Management, Water harvesting and conservation etc. will help to produce the human resource to increase the productivity of the country. Teaching sciences should lead healthy of life.

Social Upliftment

A programme on improving the social life of the community should be attempted by providing courses on empowerment of women and socially deprived; care of people at the marginal level and children and youth development.

Good Governance: Good governance is required to promote the grass-root level administration–i.e. Village Panchayat–Gram Swaraj for which we need a band of personnel with self-confidence and commitment to work in rural areas. Awareness creation and capacity building should form part of the studies on Political Science and Development Administration.

Parliamentary democracy and participatory local government will be successful only when the people are empowered to take decision, initiate and monitor the functioning of the government. Initiative for development should come from the people for which awareness creation and capacity building are essential.

Cultural Life of a Country

Culture and literature reflect the ethos and the life style of the people. This is to be preserved and disseminated to the next generation to make them feel proud of their past heritage and by adding new dimension to it through new culture, language and literature. Every student should be proud and try to imbibe the best to disseminate. This will promote spiritual power and harmony with religions, build self-confidence and civilised human being.

We need the human resources to take the knowledge and capacity accumulated at the university to the doorsteps of people in villages to build Gram Swaraj, for which a broad based curriculum model to be followed at the institutes of higher education is given. This model is given to ponder over and decide the course of study on the basis of the local requirement and availability of resources.

Curriculum at the Higher Education Level

All the three dimensions of education–Teaching, Research and Extension should reflect the needs of Society. Curriculum at the Higher Education level for Rural Development should be based on the societal needs and locale specific. Over a period of time the Institutes of higher learning have considerably modified their curriculum due to Socio, Cultural, Political and Economic pressures and the conscious efforts to make education more meaningful and have relevance. Many universities have realised the need for coming down to the reality from the concept "Ivory Tower of Learning" by making their curriculum more need based and socially relevant. They started moving towards the society with a social concern. This is the right time that all universities start thinking about modifying the curriculum at Undergraduate and Postgraduate levels. Universities should move forward by unfolding its scope to various challenges in 21st century. There is need to link its programmes with area of development in the community keeping in view its expansion and change in future. It is an unending journey.

To ensure harmonious progress of the society new courses of studies, strategies and new techniques are needed to be introduced in the institutes of higher learning for accelerated growth of the community, Educational institutions are expected to play a more meaningful role by providing proper human resources needed for different growth related programmes in the society. Well informed, trained and capacitated human resources are needed for industrial, economic, agricultural, scientific, cultural, health, commercial and material progress and development of the country. Being the apex of educational pyramid the institutes of higher education have special responsibility in fulfilling the human resource requirement.

Rural and Cottage Industries for Eradication of Poverty and Unemployment in Villages

"Mahatma Gandhi says Swadeshi is that spirit in us which requires us to serve our immediate neighbours before others, and to use things produced in our neighbourhood in preference to those more remote". (Young India: August 20, 1919)

He also says that:

> "... using foreign articles, rejecting those that are manufactured in India, is to be untrue to India. To use foreign articles because we do not like indigenous ones is to be a foreigner. It is obvious that we cannot reject the native air and the native soil, because they are inferior to foreign air and soil. (Young India: May 13, 1919).

A resolution was also passed in the Congress Session held in 1906 in Calcutta, it was resolved that Congress accords its most cordial support to the Swadeshi Movement and calls upon the people of the country to labour for its success, by making earnest and sustained efforts to promote the growth of indigenous industries and to stimulate production of indigenous articles by giving them preference over imported commodities even at some sacrifice. (History of the Congress).

It was before independence that our raw materials were sent to the foreign countries and we received the final products in the form of finished articles; whereas today the question of Swadeshi and the definition of Swadeshi are something different from what Mahatma Gandhi and the Congress defined. We try to produce goods in our own countries in big industrial units instead of seeking the services of Small Scale Industrial Units in villages. Instead of giving healthy occupations and satisfying the needs of the villagers the centralised sectors using less man power produces more and makes the prices low as compared to the prices of the articles produced by the artisans in the villages. Even locally producible articles are being taken by the large-scale industries minimising employment opportunities of the villagers. India being a very big country with large population requires more employment opportunities for the mass production. It should be production by masses. Only when employment is provided to the large number of people, buying capacity will increase. It is only through Small Scale Village Industries employment could be provided to more number of people. "Small is beautiful," says Schumacher, the Western Economist. Decentralised small industries can thrive more easily and certainly than the large-scale industries.

Different Strategies for Rural Industries for their Success

Rural Industries should especially concentrate on quality production and consumption at the local level for its survival. Those who produce must be able to consume at the local level to the maximum and through exchange of commodities to other people what is required for the villages could be obtained. This is what Mahatma Gandhi perceived; whereas the scenario of village industries today is something different. The consumption pattern of the people has changed. There is a change in the living style of the people as well. What they produce is not only for consumption but also for selling so that their expenditure on education and the recreation activities could be met. In this situation, they have to find an alternate arrangement for marketing of the articles produced in villages. Next to agriculture, village industries alone could provide the largest employment to people.

It is imperative that quality goods are produced for the consumption of others. Today, the values of products which are produced by the villagers are never assessed by the producers. They do not consume what they produce, but expect others to purchase what is being produced by the Artisans. As a result the Artisans face difficulties even for their survival.

It is only through creation of awareness for using the goods produced in the villages by both the producers and others in urban area Rural Industries can survive. Local markets should be created with the assistance of the local Panchayats and other Cooperatives to market what is being produced in villages. If the problem of marketing is solved, the problems for procurement of raw materials for the industries will be automatically solved enabling the Artisans to have a better life. If the people understand that there is a market for their quality products, naturally the quality of the articles produced will also improve.

Swadeshi Industry

Swadeshi industries are those recognised by All India Khadi and Village Industries Commission, All India Board, National Small Scale Industries Corporation, Handloom and Handicraft Development Corporation for Government. These organisations support financially as well as provide subsidy and sales rebate to the industries which are recognised by them.

There are also cottage industries which are not directly under the list of Khadi and Village Industries Commission (KVIC) but still they are recognised as Rural Industries if they come within the percapita investment of Rs. 50,000 and located in villages having population of less than twenty thousand and social benefits for the weaker sections and downtrodden. Such Swadeshi industries of cottage or tiny sector provide employment to 80 per cent of industrial labour force; the Small Scale Industries provide employment to 70 per cent of the labour force and large scale sector and multinational companies provide employment to only 3 per cent of the industrial labour force. Therefore, Swadeshi industries alone can save this country from the economic crises of poverty and unemployment.

The Swadeshi industries may not be able to compete in the world economic market in terms of fashion, finishing and cost of the products. Yet they have the required utility value and relevancy to the rural life. The following are some of the industries which have high potential and relevancy to village economy. The only requirement to make them competitive is upgrading the technology, improving the quality and placing them in appropriate levels of technological upgradation for optimising the resources and productivity.

Rural Industries

The following small-scale village industries are popular and provide employment to millions of people especially in rural areas.

(1) Khadi: Khadi Cloth production gives employment to 2 million people directly and handloom industry provide employment to 10 million people and other village industries provide employment to 8 million people, with the support of All India Khadi and Village Industries Commission and various National/State level Development Corporations. If Khadi wearing among the people can be promoted, Khadi cloth production alone can provide employment to 250 million people in Indian villages. But the total unemployed population is only 100 million people which are just half of the employment potential of Khadi industry. If the people of India make up their mind and develop Swadeshi spirit Khadi industry itself can solve the unemployment problem and the Indian villages can become self-reliant.

Introduction of appropriate technology by increasing the number of spindles used in the Charkhas will increase the income of the Spinners up to Rs. 150 per day. By using 32 Spindle Charkhas, a Spinner can earn up to Rs. 200 a day. Use of power will reduce the drudgery and increase the production.

The spinning industry can be facilitated by a technologically viable pre-processing centre consisting of a 3-beator blow room line, carding, draw frame and simple machinery.

Spinning can be operated in cottages, in the homes of the workers. The rowing input (sliver) can be obtained from the centralised pre-processing centre.

(2) Weaving: Weaving industry in Khadi sector provides employment to 10 million people in pit looms, frame looms, Nepali looms and Jacquard looms. Though the quality of the handloom products is preferred for export marketing all over the world, the labour productivity is less and the wage also is less when compared to power looms. A Power loom costs Rs. 25000; a Pit loom costs only Rs. 1000; a Nepali loom costs Rs. 10,000 and a Jacquard loom costs Rs. 15,000. Owing to the cost factor most of the weavers go for pit looms. The frame loom is an improvement over the pit loom. The Nepali loom is an improvement over the frame loom and the Jacquard loom is an improvement over the frame loom with design weaving facility.

The weaver gets tired in a few hours of weaving work. He cannot continuously weave even for eight hours. If the weavers own the looms and have them in their home other members of the family also can take part in weaving and share other activities. This will help in producing more cloth a day. When the looms are owned by the master weavers in a shed and institutions, the worker may find it difficult to weave continuously; thus the productivity will be low and the wage will also be inadequate. To increase the earnings efforts could also be taken to motorize the shuttle speed of 120 picks per minute in the Nepali looms with metal frame.

This will give a wage of Rs. 100 per day by producing about 15 meters of fabric in 8 hours. This will also reduce the drudgery of the worker as the pedaling process is eliminated. This can be installed in any cottage with proper flooring.

(3) Dyeing and Printing: The Indian villages are endowed with thousands of natural dye sources. This dyeing and printing process can be attended by women in villages. Only proper training is required to identify the dye sources and the use of dye materials. Eco friendly Natural Dye from Indigo, Turmeric, Madder, Pomegranate rind, Manjista roots, Naval seeds and Barks, Myrobolan, Karungali pattai, Vengai pattai, Tamarind and similar other vegetable sources attract the people. In fact it is becoming an attraction for exporting to the foreign countries as they are becoming more cautious of chemicals being used. The capital investment is less than Rs. 50000 and employment can be generated for six to eight persons in a family who can work at home itself.

(4) Oil Industry: The portable power Ghani which is already approved by Khadi and Village Industries Commission is an ideal model for oil seed crushing industry. Attachment of in-built oil filter in the Ghani will make the extraction of pure oil easier. The capital investment will be Rs. 1,00,000 per unit of two ghanis with adequate working capital. This will give employment for four persons in a family with a daily wage of Rs. 120 per person. This process can be attended by the women also as complete mechanisation has been done in the crushing process.

(5) Soap Industry: Soap making is the most suited cottage industry which does not require any electricity in the process. Capital investment is about Rs. 1,00,000 for equipments including working capital. This industry can give employment to five to six persons in a family with an average income of Rs. 150 per person per day.

(6) Handmade Paper Industry: Handmade paper industry uses agricultural waste, hosiery cuttings, rags, press cuttings and any fibrous material which are available in villages as well as in urban areas. The capital investment for this industry is around Rs. 10. 00 lakhs for a village level small-scale unit, which can provide employment to 20 men and women. Average income will be Rs. 150 per person per day. There is a very high scope for paper conversion products. This will in future substitute the plastic carry bags for packing of materials.

(7) Bakery: Bakery is a highly growing small-scale industry with an investment of about Rs. 50,000 for a cottage unit. The cottage unit can be run with Brick Oven built indigenously. The industry can use locally available millets like Ragi, Bajra, Jowar, Maize, etc., in addition to Wheat as the main products. Use of local agricultural produce in Bakery industry can create better marketing for local agricultural resources. A Bakery unit can employ 5-6 persons in a family with a small investment.

(8) Fruit Preservation and Processing: Plenty of fruits grow in India. Fruit growing cannot be a profitable venture unless it is processed and preserved all through the year. Fruits as seasonal and perishable commodity need to be preserved for use throughout the year. Owing to its perishable nature and seasonal availability, price fluctuation is unpredictable in fruit growing industry. This industry can provide employment opportunity especially to village women if they are trained to preserve fruits. Common fruits like Tomato, Grapes, Orange, Lemon, Papaya, Banana, Guava, Pineapple and Jack fruits are available in plenty during the seasons. We need salt free water (soft water). Capital investment will be Rs. 1.00 lakh per unit at the village level and can provide employment to 10 women/men who on an average can earn Rs. 120 per day respectively.

(9) Processing of Cereals and Pulses: Cereals and Pulses are also available in season. When the Cereals and Pulses are sold as raw products, the farmers will get only less income. When they are processed and preserved it will be profitable. When Ragi is processed into ragi malt it could be sold at Rs. 120 per kg. There is a margin up to Rs. 100 per kg as profit and other intermediate overheads. If this is processed in a same village, the transport cost is reduced owing to employment generation in the same village. Similar value addition can be noticed in Bajra, Maize and other millets. While processing and preserving nutrients could also be added.

(10) Cottage Industries for Kerala: Besides the above mentioned industries, Kerala could concentrate on Palm industry, where Palmyra and Coconut trees are in abundance in Kerala Neem, Sugar and Crystals could be prepared for consuming directly and other cottage industries like making Coir products, Spoons and other products, Coconut shells, etc. Climbing devices could be used to climb large number of trees, for earning more. This device will also reduce the drudgery of the workers.

Masala powder making, papad making, fiber products, low cost building materials, poultry, dairy, herbal products, mushroom cultivation, bio-gas, solar energy equipments, bee-keeping, honey processing, sericulture are some of the village based industries which are to be promoted with appropriate technology with low capital investment aiming at higher employment generation and higher purchasing power in the hands of the people. The Swadeshi industries with appropriate technology alone can solve the problem of poverty and unemployment in Indian villages as the big industrial sector which engages only 3 per cent of the labour force in India.

28

Tourism Development and Alleviation of Rural Poverty

"There was something living and dynamic about this heritage which showed itself in ways of living and a philosophical attitude to life and its problems. Ancient India ..... was a world in itself, a culture and civilisation which gave shape to all things." Jawaharlal Nehru thus states in his "The Discovery of India."

The secret of this dynamic civilisation lies in India's capacity to accommodate and absorb different customs and fuse them into a wholesome culture. India being a vast and diverse country has something to offer to everyone. The beauty of its ancient monuments, the beat and rhythm of its folk ands classical dance, its colourful bazaars, its charming people, its elegant architecture and above all its timeless appeal have made India virtually a tourists' paradise.

In this fast changing world people are constantly mobile either for education or employment. Prosperity, leisure coupled with the quest for pleasure and knowledge has been the motivating factors that promote mobility and subsequently tourism. Tourism has become a complex phenomenon today. To achieve greater degree of achievement, in our economy through tourism the focus should be on the development of our entrepreneurship programmes, both economic and social; create more jobs for rural poor through tourism. There are high hopes and a common interest in revival of rural economy. Travel is a powerful force for providing economic growth, rural development and alleviation of poverty as it brings people with varied interest together.

Besides economic benefits to a country by way of earning foreign exchange and employment generation, tourism makes a tremendous contribution to cultural exchange, social improvement and political understanding. It is not a fringe activity any more. It is a promotion of cultural exchange and international cooperation. Popularly known as an 'industry without chimneys' tourism is one of the best means of earning revenues, being a labour intensive as well as capital intensive industry. In developing countries like India, promotion of tourism is absolutely necessary not only to promote social and political understanding but also to generate lucrative employment opportunities and to alleviate rural poverty.

A stream of benefits can flow from tourism into rural economy in the form of wages, rentals or lease for the use of tourists during the seasons. Tourism also helps the local people who provide services such as craftsmen, building maintenance, and other small business activities and promote seasonal employment. Thus the tourism changes the quality of life of the local people.

Madurai-a City with Potential for Tourism

Madurai, a city of temple and ancient culture has been a centre of attraction for tourists inside and outside India. This city which is a monument of Pandya culture not only stands as a monument for architecture but is also renowned for handicrafts and art, now for education and social service activities.

There are various types of tourism and Madurai District almost offers all varieties. For Monument tourism and we have Thirumalai Naicker Mahal; Gandhi Museum, for Mountain tourism we have many hills ideal for trekking; for culture tourism, where else do we get evidence for diverse culture if not in Madurai with its Hindu temples, Churches and Dharkas; for business tourism Madurai is famous for various business transactions including the famous Sungudi sarees; there is a particular tourism purely meant to give sensuous pleasure, our Kodai Hills is a "thing of beauty which is a joy for ever"; above all there is spiritual tourism and Madurai witnesses thousands of pilgrims every year from within and without India. When Madurai has so much to offer to tourists, it can definitely be of a great source of rural development and cause for poverty alleviation.

Tourism Promoters

A few factors that are elemental for tourism promotion are—(1) pleasing weather; (2) scenic attraction; (3) historical and cultural factors; (4) accessibility; (5) amenities; (6) accommodation and other amenities, food; and (7) Transport.

Climate is of particular significance to tourism and there are many areas in and around Madurai with exhilarating and salubrious climate. Similarly scenic attractions are in plenty; Madurai justly boasts of a historical and cultural past and it is accessible by road, rail and air. When we have almost all these facilities why cannot we make long term, sustainable plans to encourage rural enterprises?. Planning of tourism and rural development should be linked to urban planning. What is produced in rural areas should be displayed and marketed in urban areas.

Tourists are our Guests

Tourists are not only a source of income; they are our guests. 'Adithi Devo Bhava', a guest is like a god. Indian mythology swarms with stories of great hospitality. India has been a gourmets' paradise through ages. The villages of South India are famous for their special delicacies and the spices and varieties have always been gourmets' delight. Apart from special barbecues arranged for the pleasure of other guests in which the chefs from villages-not Cordon Blue Chefs-could be invited to display their culinary skills, they can be employed permanently in our restaurants.

The folk artists could feast the eyes and ears of the tourists. Oyillattam, Mayilattam, Karagattam and Thevarattam of Tamil Nadu with their rhythm and movement have been perennial source of delight to every one. Slowly we are forgetting these folk arts and the artists in rural area are dwindling in number. Revival of these arts is essential for poverty alleviation as well as cultural revival. By doing so, on the one hand we develop and revive our art and on the other we help our village artists with substantial income.

The Cotton products including sarees are comparatively cheaper; but the quality is always maintained in this part of the country. There are instances where wholesale purchase is made of these products and sold in urban shops at exorbitant prices. The rich become richer as the poor remain poor. These weavers and artisans should be given chances to display and market their wares directly to tourists for a reasonable profit by establishing showrooms exclusively for them. Even-distribution of wealth will automatically lead to poverty alleviation. These arrangements will encourage the small entrepreneurs to come out with better and attractive designs and productions.

There is a positive correlation between growth of tourism and increase in the level of employment permanent as well as seasonal employment. The youth from villages, educated but unemployed could be trained to become tourist guides and also receptionists. They are the sons of the soil and have imbibed the tradition and culture of our villages. They need training in communication skills, commitment and admiration of our cultural and social ethos.

There are instances where private sectors make huge profits out of selling the handicrafts and souvenir items like palm products, ornamental items, herbal medicinal items, carvings in stone and wood, Jewellery manufactured by the rural artisans. These rural manufacturers can be given an opportunity to directly market their products so that they get the benefit directly. The Self-Help Groups organised by women should be encouraged to come out of their shells of domestic duties and channelise their potential and market their products. This will not only help in developing rural economy but also enable the rural mass, especially women, to be aware of the society around them and be successful entrepreneurs. The gap between the rural and urban populace will also narrow down.

To Promote Tourism-Suggestions

The possibilities are wide and numerous to promote tourism through which poverty in rural area be alleviated. But we have to be realistic and practical too. The first step towards this is we have to acknowledge that there is absolute necessity to make our environment clean and eco-friendly so that tourists come to us with a feeling of security. There is need to modernize our transport facilities. The tourists, especially from abroad, are used to certain luxuries and comforts. These may appear as luxuries to us; but to them it is their way of life and we are obliged to provide these to them if we want to promote tourism. Taste of real and original India does not mean 'dust and dirt' but 'tradition and hospitality'. It is our duty to make the "adhithi" comfortable. Our roads, airports and railways are not up to the global standards though "Globalisation" has become a password every where. Resource Management and service delivery should be strategically devised and implemented to attract the tourists to our place.

To Conclude

We have achieved so much in the past in promoting tourism. We are achieving so much in the present also. The few suggestions given above are viable, feasible, and achievable. The Sergeant Committees' recommendation was that "the work of development of tourist traffic in India should be undertaken on a methodical basis by a separate organisation". Tourist Traffic Branch was set up and various aspects of tourism are being taken care of. Tourists pour into India and we have thought about having posh hotels to accommodate them, arranging for tours etc for them. This has become an established industry. Let us now think and plan for making use of this industry for rural development and rural poverty alleviation.

29

UN and Global Peace

Turning and turning in the widening gyre

The falcon cannot hear the falconer;

Things fall apart, the centre cannot hold;

Mere anarchy is loosed upon the world

—W.B. Yeats 'The Second Coming'

What Yeats said about modern civilisation nearly three decades ago is an evidence of his prophetic vision. In this age of Science and Technology where man is to be at his most civilised we see only blood shed, violence and 'anarchy' let loose on the world. On the one hand we boast of growth and development; on the other we witness deterioration of moral values. Unless a new social order is formed, unless fraternity is fostered and unless man realises the value of culture and tradition we will be hurtling towards doom. This state of affairs has not just affected a single state, a single country or a single continent. Violence and terrorism have taken hold of the entire globe affecting the lives of human beings who live in perpetual fear and uncertainty.

A Buddha is born only once, a Jesus appears only once, a Gandhi is sent by God only once as saviors of mankind.

They had lived for the humanity and shed their blood for peace. At least in the memory of such great souls it is high time the whole humanity united to fight against terrorism and violence.

United Nations and Global Peace

Many organisations with the sole objective of bringing peace and prosperity to humanity have come up and are functioning effectively. One such organisation is the U.N. The founding fathers of the United Nations, in designing its structure and function brought to bear preconceptions about international relations which predated the Second World War and the nuclear age.

The primary objective of the United Nations is the maintenance of international peace and security, the pacific settlement of international disputes and the establishment of international cooperation. The U.N. Charter obligates the member-states to settle their disputes through peaceful means and when these attempts prove futile the Security Council and General Assembly are called to intervene.

The United Nations came into being on October 24, 1945 with 51 nations as members with the major desire to 'save future generations from the scourge of war'. The purposes of its Charter are as follows:

1. To maintain international peace and security and to take effective collective measures for the prevention and removal of threats to peace.....,
2. to develop friendly relations among nations based on principles of equal rights,
3. to achieve international cooperation in solving economic, social and cultural problems, and
4. to be a centre for harmonising the actions of nations in the attainment of these common ends.

The United Nations has made commendable achievement in its prime objective of maintaining international peace. To cite a few instances; the very first case that came before the U.N. Security Council was from Iran regarding Soviet interference in the internal affairs of Iran. Through the successful negotiations of the U.N., the Soviet troops withdrew from the Iranian soil.

When the Dutch continued to occupy Indonesia and initiated military actions against Indonesia the Security Council appointed a Committee of Good Office and a truce plan was signed between Holland and Indonesia. When Holland violated the pact it was again the U.N. which intervened and Indonesia got its independence and became a member of U.N. in 1950.

But there are cases where the U.N. has not been able to solve the conflicts between the nations involved. Kashmir issue is a dispute, which has been in the agenda of the U.N. since 1948. Though many Commissions have been set up to bring peace to the region by declaring a peace pact and insisting on 'cease-fire' the smoldering fires of hatred have never ceased to exist. Cross-Border terrorism continues to exist. Cross-border infiltration is in increase but one cannot deny the fact that without the intervention of the U.N. Kashmir problem could have precipitated a major international crisis.

Similarly the Palestine-Israel-Arab conflict remains unsolved despite being on the agenda of United Nations. Durable peace is still a mirage in these nations. As Palmer and Perkins rightly pointed out the conflict between North and South Korea precipitated "the greatest international crisis since the end of World War II". Despite the great efforts of the U.N. the crisis still remains unsolved. The efforts of the U.N. have not borne fruit in Suez crisis too. The Congo-Belgian Conflict though resolved by the UN, later on led to 'internal grab for power' that destroyed the peace of the common people of Congo. The mandate of the U.N. to maintain Congo's territorial integrity and political independence succeeded for a short time. Once the U.N.

withdrew its forces from Congo, Civil war broke out. The Congo operation was one of the gravest responsibilities shouldered by the U.N.

If the U.N. has failed in its peace mission in many cases it has also succeeded in settling many international disputes. As long as there is power politics and as long as man yearns for supremacy no single organisation can completely succeed in bringing about global peace. It is imperative that every individual has to be made aware of his responsibilities. Only drops collect to make an ocean. The ocean of U.N. needs the collective endeavours of every man, every nation and every continent.

U.N. could also identify the Nations with terrorists and isolate them. Terrorists should not be given asylum in any part of the world. Such countries should be declared as terrorist state and be expelled from U.N. No fund from any source for the developmental activities of these countries is provided. U.N. should make all countries feel the responsibility of protecting the world from the terrorism.

India's Contribution to Promote Peace

There have been advocates of peace in every nation. Mahatma Gandhi was perhaps the world's foremost advocate and exemplar of non-violent methods and peace in this century. He was the Apostle of Peace. He was the inspiring symbol of the peace and harmony on the earth. His principle of satyagraha as a means of conflict resolution came to be widely recognised and attracted people world wide. Gandhi was often asked whether he was a saint or a politician. He replied that the word saint was too sacred to be lightly applied to someone like him and that he was "a humble searcher of truth". The harmonious transformation of relationship between England and India in 1947 was the result of Gandhian method of non-violence and an evidence of the success of non-violent approach. In the history of mankind there have been so many turning points, when old was replaced by the new. To bring about peace to the world a new praxis is needed and Gandhi has a lot to offer.

Similarly the 'Dream' of Martin Luther King who envisaged the close of racial discrimination and the dawn of brotherhood where people lived as one whole should become a reality. There should be a global peace movement. The movement should be at a global level and not at a regional, ethnic or national level and should be at the highest level so far experienced by any social movement. At this movement of globalisation this should be made possible.

Already there is a growing awareness among the people of all nations about the menace of arms race and the need for disarmament. From the conceptual level this should be elevated to the practical level. This global peace movement should involve every human being towards disarmament. This movement should transcend national, territorial borders and aim at bringing the humanity under a single but multicolored umbrella of love, compassion, mutual respect and brotherhood make every one feel that "earth is but one country and man kind its citizen"-a borderless world. This movement should target at universal suffrage, women rights and literacy for all. The most distinguishing feature of this movement is its non-centralised organisational character. Modeled on Gandhian principles this movement should be a bridge between spirituality and politics. One global culture, one global consciousness, one global spirituality should be the motto of this movement. Nothing is 'yours' or 'mine', everything becomes 'ours'.

The initiation, financial and moral support can be rendered by United Nations. As pointed out earlier the U.N. might have failed, in certain cases in peace making but its efforts at peace keeping have met with certain measures of success. Its attempts at peace making have been hampered by the political disputes between East and West, lack of clear charter mandate. Despite the severe constraints the U.N. has been carrying on its noble mission of maintaining international peace. The global peace movement will be an added force to the U.N. The world is moving away from a state centric model of society towards cross-national model. Establishment of US Institute of Peace is a milestone in global peace movement. The University for Peace, located at Costa

Rica is an International institution devoted to seeking peace through education with humanistic purposes and according to the principles of charter of the United Nations and the universal Declaration of Human Rights. Placed outside the organisational framework of the U.N. but at the same time not simply a national project, the University for Peace is particularly suited to deal with the problem of human survival through justice and peace. Similar attempts should be made in the institutions of higher learning through out the globe to expose people to the global peace.

Educationists, politicians, administrators, scholars, farmers, common men and women should join hands and become a part of the global peace movement and strengthen the hands of the United Nations which function solely towards international peace. The 'anarchy let loose' should disappear, the things that are falling apart should be firmly held by a centre which can hold and strengthened by strivers of peace and harmony. A new social order, when men and women from various parts of the globe live in peace and harmony should arise out of the cold ashes of violence. From the dictionary words like terrorism, insecurity, violence should disappear. This is not an idle dream, but a possible reality. Humankind can achieve anything if there is a will. Let us look forward to a world of peace and harmony, sunshine and smiles!.

30

Towards a Peaceful and Just Society without Violence

> "I have embraced the non-violent—resistance technique in fighting for freedom because I am convinced it is the only legitimate and humane way"
>
> —***Chief Albert Luthuli***

As Science and Technology advance and develop the whole world shrinks and hence it has become imperative that human beings live together in harmony in this global village. But what do we see today? Forces of hatred and violence are let loose and rampant. Instead of using science and technology for advancement we tend to use them for destruction. Respect for human life and human value is slowly being replaced by egotism and avarice for power, for money and for glory. The twenty first century has seen the dawn of violence whereas it should have been the dawn of civilisation with prosperity, progress and peace in the society. If mankind had started using its achievement in the field of science and technology, rich culture, arts, spiritual pursuit and intellectual caliber of every nation would have spread joy, happiness and peace every where. To quote Sri Aurobindo who addressed the nation on 15th August, 1947, the day on which India got her independence,-"I have always held and said that India was arising, not to serve her own material interests only, to achieve expansion, greatness, power and prosperity-though these two she must not neglect and certainly not like others to acquire domination of other people, but to live also for God and the world as a helper and leader of the whole human race". We wish to move towards this direction without bloodshed.

Origins of Violence

Violence is not originally an external force. It starts in the minds of the individuals. When man starts thinking of amasing wealth and power to promote his own self he goes to any extent in order to achieve this and shuts out every other being and values. The love for power to get a better status and position in the society and; the bid for wealth to enjoy the pleasures of luxury these have become the twin goals in the world. Racial discrimination, social distinctions, and religious fanaticism add fuel to fire and breed conflicts and mistrust in the minds of men. The pomp and show of the rich on the one hand and squalor and hunger of the poor on the other hand, the material prosperity of a minority and the abysmal despair of the majority—imbalances such as these galore paving way to frustration and ultimately violence. Man lives in perpetual fear of his life. Anarchy is let loose. The concepts of sathya dharma and vinaya go into a state of oblivion. Many of the violations of human rights are the result of suspicion, lack of trust and loss of cultural values. Man uses his intellect not to cultivate good will and peace but to breed violence and terrorism, thus destroy the peace in the world.

Violence-a Tool of Terrorism

In order to strike fear in the minds of people terrorists resort to violence as a powerful weapon. Now-a-days terrorism is not just confined to a nation; it has crossed borders, not even which, terrorism is borderless. Terrorists are in need of armaments and this involves money. Through violent means terrorists function at various levels. Using physical menace they rob people, nations and ultimately it spreads through the entire globe. There is violence at all levels-at social level, political level, and cultural level and even at religious level. Great religious leaders like Christ and Budda preached non-violence and ahimsa and in the land of their birth there is terrorism, war and bloodshed. Great political leaders like Gandhi, Vinobha and Nehru advocated peace and non-violence to create a joyful and just society. Their land is invaded by terrorists who use violence to intimidate people.

Type of Violence

The main form of violence is intimidation through physical violence. Arson, armed, robbery and Bomb culture have become part and parcel of human life. Hijacking and kidnapping have become every day occurrences. Breeding fear in the minds of people through bloodshed is a byword in the dictionary of terrorists. There is violence in the emotional level. Blackmailing and posing threats to the lives of kith and kin and annihilation of values drain people emotionally and violate the sense of security. The physical and emotional insecurity ultimately leads to intellectual deterioration. When one goes in perpetual fear of his life, when one goes in perpetual emotional denial his intellect also gets blunt. The loss of human values, the loss of cultural heritage, and the loss of traditional norms ultimately shake the foundations of spiritualism thus creating spiritual violence. The strongest weapon of terrorists, violence, abuses the lives of many innocent people on physical, emotional, intellectual and spiritual level and subsequently people are demoralised and the terrorists are able to achieve their ends easily.

Advocates of Non-violence

Our India is a land of seers and sages. Great people like Gandhi, Nehru, Tagore, Ramakrishna Paramahamsa have left their foot prints on the sands of time. They have been our spiritual and moral leaders. They taught us kindness and justice tempered with mercy will be the most effective antidote to violence as violence begets only violence. Americans, the world's most powerful nation in the world, today lives in fear of terrorism after 11th September 2001 and have no peace of mind even for a minute though they possess everything to destroy the whole world in a fraction of a second. When India was under British colonisation, none more passionately wanted freedom than Gandhiji, yet he asked his fellowmen not to harm even "one hair of one head of Englishmen". His aim was not to defeat the British but to effect a change of heart. His concern was more for freedom of spirit than political independence and that was why at the eve of Independence. Nehru and Lord Mountbatten shared the same platform in genuine friendship and ever-lasting bond of love. People like Martin Luther King dreamed about a state where Black boys and White boys will hold hands and live in peace and harmony. Even in the face of racial discrimination, and searing flames of injustice Martin Luther King sought justice through a peace march. Dalai Lama accomplished a powerful and lasting social influence without picking up a weapon of bloodshed. He chose nonviolent spiritual force that is mightier than any other weapon. Even while being crucified Jesus Christ pleaded for the sinners. Such great people are still revered not because of material prosperity or political power but for their love of humanity. They were the advocates of peace through non-violent means; a permanent and everlasting spiritual force when wielded with moral strength will put terrorism to shame.

Means to Moral Strength-Education an Instrument

A Gandhi is born only once, so is a Jesus, a Buddha. But lesser mortals like all of us should contribute our mite to fight against terrorism and violence for peaceful co-existence. To achieve this right kind of education is to be provided. It is an instrument which shapes the destiny of people. Education lights the lamp of knowledge dispelling darkness and ignorance. Gita says "Education imparts intellectual culture; it secures capacity and stability. Capacity and stability enable one to secure wealth-wealth to conform to Dharma which leads to ultimate peace and happiness." The right type of education is the key to peace and prosperity leading to a just society. Right type of education inspires one with confidence, inculcates moral values, fosters social stability, gives prosperity and ultimately teaches the values of fraternity and love for everyone. Has not our national poet Tagore prayed for knowledge that is free, and for strength to raise the mind high above daily trifles, for tireless striving towards perfection and for a mind that is without fear. Only education makes this a reality. Young students in the institutes of higher education should be encouraged to sit for a dialogue with their peers from all over the world along with their role models in the society. There should be fruitful interaction on common problems and finding solutions to them. Vidya means learning or scholarship the first step of which is humility. One should humble oneself on this earth and shed the greed for material prosperity. Education will provide one with necessary accessories towards developing a fearless mind and accepting all as equals. Spiritual values will sharpen intellectual values. Materialism will bow before truth; cultural values will establish the right kind of pride. And education is the only instrument which can lead to all these. Totally committed teachers could be the spiritual leaders of the young minds light the minds with the lamp of knowledge. Every one should understand the futility of :

- Politics without principle
- Pleasure without conscience
- Commerce without morality
- Knowledge without character
- Science without humanity
- Wealth without work and
- Worship without sacrifice

When one realises this he will rise above all material things and strive for humanism and help to achieve a social order with peace, justice and harmony. Let us march towards that horizon and guide our youth towards that goal.

Conclusion

'Non man as an island' as Donne has said. As said earlier science and technology has made it possible for men to live in close communion. In such a situation men should live in peace and harmony. What we see now is violence and terrorism. If we wake up every day with uncertainty about our future what kind life are we leading? Instead of destroying the lives of others around us for selfish motives let us try to live in peace and harmony. Education will equip us with necessary values to counteract and combat violence and terrorism. Human life is precious, priceless and a gift of god. Let us "wait and watch at the way side where light chases shadow and rain comes in the wake of summer", let the evil days of violence end and the world see the dawn of peace and harmony! This is my dream, this is my prayer and this will be a reality soon. Yes.

We shall over come someday

Deep in my heart I do believe

We shall overcome someday.

31

Satyagraha as an Alternative to Terrorism

Terrorism has become a byword these days. Many, especially the modern youth, try to justify terrorism as a means for restoring social justice to those who have turned frustrated in the face of disappointments in life. The popular image of terrorists is that of fearless men/women who are capable of any extremes. Terrorists are portrayed as strong men and women in relentless pursuit of their goal and in this pursuit of their goal they do not hesitate to wipe out anyone whom they feel are detrimental to their reaching their goal. But as Gandhiji has said, "terrorism is a weapon not of the strong but of the weak"-the morally, psychologically weak who do not have the strength or will power to resist temptation–temptation to destroy, temptation to kill, temptation to prove their physical superiority.

Is terrorism the only way to eradicate social injustice? By resorting to terrorism are we not encouraging evil? Is there not a positive way for the people to get social justice and live in peace? The father of our nation had been living proof to show that through Satyagraha the most important revolutionary contribution to achieve political, economic and social freedom, one can achieve the goal without blood shed, violence and hatred. Satyagraha has been designed as an effective substitute for violence, by following truth and non-violence.

Whereas terrorism is targeted against people, satyagraha is targeted against injustice; whereas a terrorist make enemies, a satyagrahi loves his so called enemy and owns no enemy; whereas a terrorist chooses to fight with destructive weapons, a satyagrahi strives to reach the reason through the heart; whereas a terrorist is blinded by self love and is intolerant, a satyagrahi has infinite patience, abundant faith in others and ample hope; whereas a terrorist is motivated by cynicism and violence, a satyagrahi has no other stay but God and is optimistic; whereas a terrorist is filled with hatred and is ready to make others suffer, a satyagrahi knows no limit in his capacity for suffering, he would neither retaliate nor would he submit to the criminal, but seek to cure him by curing himself; whereas a terrorist poses to have courage, a satyagrahi possesses moral courage to resist evil.

Basically satyagraha means, "having faith in conducting life in a truthful manner". It is a method of resisting injustice by controlling body, speech and mind. The concept of satyagraha is three pronged–(i) 'sat" which implies openness, honesty and fairness; (ii) ahimsa which implies refusal to inflict injury on others; (iii) tapasya which implies willingness for self-sacrifice.

A person can turn into terrorist overnight because it is easy to take a weapon against the fellow human being. But it takes time to become a satyagrahi because he should be willing to shoulder any sacrifice which is occasioned by the struggle which he has initiated rather than pursuing such sacrifice onto his opponent. The goal of the satyagrahi is to discover a wider vista of truth and justice, not to achieve victory over the opponent.

Today's youth are easily influenced by the media which portrays a hero who takes law into his own hands and destroys evil men, and becomes the saviour of the downtrodden. True, the picture is attractive–but only on the superficial level. Our war should be against evil not against evil men; against wickedness and not the wicked. Annihilation of people will never help in achieving peace and tranquility; there is always a sense of guilt, which again leads to a sense of frustration. When the war is against corruption and evil the goal is positive; there is a sense of achievement and the soul is filled with serenity. Only through nonviolence and satyagraha one can achieve this end.

The weapon of a satyagrahi is passive resistance. "It is an all-sided sword which can be used anyhow. It blesses him who uses it against whom it is used. Without drawing a drop of blood it produces far-reaching results. It never rusts and cannot be stolen". Was not Gandhiji a living example? He won the reverence and admiration of not only the British, but also the entire world by using the weapon of passive resistance. If the Britishers are today our friends it because of Gandhi's satyagraha. If we had resorted to terrorism, we would have ended up making enemies of the Britishers and ultimately the whole world. If India is looked up as a model to be emulated it is because of our infinite tolerance and compassion. But lo! Even we are slowly being invaded by terrorism and falling into the clutches of terrorists.

Passive resistance, nonviolence or satyagraha does not mean that one has to be passive under duress. The Buddha fearlessly carried the war into the enemy's camp and brought down on its knees an arrogant priesthood. Christ drove out the money changers from the temple of Jerusalem and drew down curses from Heaven upon the hypocrites. Both were intensely direct actions. But even as Buddha and Christ chastised, they showed unmistakable gentleness and love behind every act of theirs. They would never surrender the truth for which they lived.

Similarly a satyagrahy treats Civil disobedience as his right. He does not turn violence against others; but proves his infinite capacity for suffering and ultimately wins the war through peace. His is a yudh, a dharma yudh and not a destructive terrorism.

Why go far back seeking samples in the lives of Buddha and Christ? Don't we have the visionary Martin Luther King who led the procession of hundreds and thousands of Black Americans to realise his dream that his "four little children will one day live in a nation where they will not be judged by the colour of their skin but by content of their character ... that one day every valley shall be exalted, every hill and mountain shall be made low...." In the annals of American history the Civil Rights Movement of Martin Luther King will remain forever as a glorious curtain raiser for passive resistance, in other words satyagraha. King called himself the disciple of Mahathma Gandhi and emulated his model.

I have just one appeal to make to the youth of today. Do not justify terrorism as a fight against social injustice; do not resort to terrorism when you come across disappointments in life'.

'You may encounter defeats, But you are NOT defeated'

A terrorist turns his weapon against a politician, an industrialist, a socialist, a businessman. He does not stop to think of these people as fathers, husbands, sons and above all human beings. No one has the right to take the life of another human being. We would not have lost our dynamic, young Prime Minister, Rajiv Gandhi if the terrorists had considered for a minute that they were terminating the life of a human being at his prime. Had Bin Laden realised that hundreds were the innocent victims of his mindless frenzy he would not have resorted to violence. Now he is a fugitive whose life is at stake. Violence breeds only violence.

'Satyagraha is utter self-effacement, greatest humiliation, greatest patience and brightest faith. It is its own reward!. The reward may take time for fruition. Satyagraha is a force that works silently, and apparently slowly. Have patience, have faith, the reward will come surely. It is a positive reward which fills your heart with absolute peace, ultimate happiness. There is no guilt as wrought by terrorism. Satyagraha gives you utmost freedom, freedom of soul, freedom from negativity. Terrorism binds you, forever to the hell of suffering through a sense of guilt and evil

Be morally strong and be a satyagrahi in pursuit of truth through non-violence rather than a terrorist who uses intimidation and violence against others and ultimately the predator becomes a prey. But a satyagrahi is not swayed by evil passions and the halo of truth and honesty protects him from evil forces and his weapon is a–weapon of love and peace that is everlasting!

32

A Disabled-Friendly Campus of Higher Education

Preamble

Indian society is hierarchical and stratified. It is stratified on the basis of caste and creed, language and occupation. Disability, physical and mental, is yet another factor which divides our Indian society sharply. In other words, the disabled in India are pushed to the fringes of our society and are systematically excluded from the mainstream.

India was the first signatory in South Asia, to the proclamation on the full participation and equality of people with disabilities in the Asian Pacific Decade of Disabled Persons 1993-2002. The main objective of the proclamation was the need to improve the living condition of persons with disabilities by providing them with equal opportunity for learning, employment, protection of rights and full participation.

It is high time that the disabled are rehabilitated and are brought to the mainstream and it becomes the responsibility of the public and the private organisations. Both should join together in implementing a comprehensive programme for the disabled. Students with disabilities have many capabilities that have not been tapped. We have to develop a new perspective and vision so that the dreams of the disabled are fulfilled and at the same time they are brought into the mainstream.

Individuals with disability can contribute positively to their families, institutions, friends and communities if we provide a disabled-friendly atmosphere in the educational institutions. They need greater opportunities for educational programmes that will identify, highlight and build upon their strengths. This will enable them to act on their own preferences and will promote their self-confidence to face the world boldly forgetting their disability. Students with disabilities can contribute and take part in nation-building activities.

S.C. Handa in "Disability Provision in India" notes, "A 1991 survey indicated that about 1.9 per cent of the population has a physical or sensory disability, and other surveys indicate that 2-2.5 per cent has a learning disability. The situation is complicated by the fact that, about 80 per cent of the disabled in India lives in rural areas, where, few facilities are available." (18)

Methodologically, it is better to clarify the terms 'disability' and 'disabled person'. Disability is defined as the "characteristic of a person that is a limitation or loss of a part of the body or mental capacity that significantly limits his or her ability to carry out some activities of independent living" (Building Design for Handicapped and Aged Persons 218).

The Persons with Disabilities Act 1995 describes a "Person with disability" as "a person suffering from not less than forty per cent of any disability as certified by a medical authority" (I:2:t). The same Act throws light on various types and dimensions of disability. The Act clarifies that :

"'**Disability**' means: (i) Blindness (ii) Low vision (iii) Leprosy-cured (iv) Hearing impairment (v) Locomotors disability (vi) Mental retardation (vii) Mental illness".

Education of the Disabled

The educational status of the physically and mentally disabled in India is very disheartening because only a very meager percentage of these sections enter the portals of a university or college. The reasons are various: First, a sizable section of the disabled are pushed to the frontiers of our society and are denied access to education. Second, the socio-economic status of the families of the disabled cannot afford higher education for their children. Third, the educational institutions themselves are not architecturally barrier-free and disabled-friendly. Four, the motivation level of the disabled students is low and many do not harbour and nurse dreams of earning a university diploma or degree.

Disability limits access to education and employment and leads to economic and social isolation. An appropriate education along with concurrent developmental programmes will play a supportive and meaningful role in this rehabilitation process. Significantly, education here would include not only the education of the disabled but the sensitisation of the general public towards disability-related issues as well.

Handa's observation merits quoting here: "Worryingly, only about five per cent of children with severe disabilities in India receive basic education. The first special schools for the disabled were set up in the 1880s, and the current number is about 3,000. However, in most of these special schools the infrastructure and standards of education are rather poor. For the most part, children with severe disabilities would attend special schools. However, the idea of integrated education—or 'mainstreaming'—is also gaining ground" ("Disability Provision in India" 18).

Against this backdrop, it has to be noted that the Persons with Disabilities Act 1995 and the University Grants Commission have taken bold steps to educate and empower the physically and mentally disabled by ensuring that the atmosphere in the educational institutions as well as the curriculum and pedagogy suit the psycho-social needs and status of the physically and mentally disabled.

The Persons with Disabilities Act envisages a lot of innovative and far-reaching programmes in Chapter V entitled "Education".

The chapter notes that "the Governments and local authorities shall :

- ensure that every child with a disability has access to free education in an appropriate environment till he attains the age of eighteen years;
- endeavour to promote the integration of students with disabilities in the normal school;
- promote setting up of special schools in Government and private sector for those in need of special education, in such a manner that children with disabilities living in any part of the country have access to such schools;
- endeavour to equip the special schools for children with disabilities with vocational training facilities."

It also discusses "Comprehensive Education Scheme". It notes that "the appropriate governments should by notification prepare a comprehensive education scheme which shall make provisions for :

- transport facilities to the children with disabilities or in the alternative financial incentives to parents or guardians to enable their children with disabilities to attend schools;
- the removal of architectural barriers from schools, colleges or other institutions imparting vocational and professional training;

- the supply of books, uniforms and other materials to children with disabilities attending school;
- the grant of scholarship to students with disabilities;
- setting up of appropriate forum for the redressal of grievances of parents regarding the placement of their wards with disabilities;
- suitable modification in the examination system to eliminate purely mathematical questions for the benefit of blind students and students with low vision;
- restructuring of curriculum for the benefit of students with disabilities;
- restructuring the curriculum for the benefit of students with hearing impairment to facilitate them to take only one language as part of their curriculum."

The UGC introduced in 1998 two schemes to enable the physically disabled in Colleges and Universities to pursue higher education: "Scheme to assist Universities/Colleges to facilitate Teacher Preparation in Special Education (TEPSE)" and "Higher Education for Persons (Disabled) with Special Needs (HEPSN)." The objectives of the Scheme are:

- To encourage Universities/Colleges of Education in India to promote teacher preparation programmes in the field of special education;
- To provide equal educational opportunities and experiences to disabled persons in higher education institutions;
- To create awareness among the functionaries of higher education about the specific educational needs of persons with disabilities;

- To equip the higher education institutions with the facilities to provide access to disabled persons;
- To provide appropriate financial assistance to disabled individuals to increase their sustainability in higher education;
- To explore suitable placement for the educated disabled graduates in public as well as in private sector enterprises; and
- To monitor the implementation of all existing and future legislation and policies pertaining to higher education of persons with disabilities."

The UGC has established Disability Units under the scheme "Higher Education for (Persons) for Disabled with Special Needs (HEPSN)" in ten institutions in our country with the following objectives:

- Facilitate admission to persons with disability. Collect regularly on annual basis information in course-wise admissions of disabled candidates in Universities/Colleges;
- Provide guidance and counseling to disabled individuals;
- Create awareness among the public about the needs of the disabled person in higher education;
- Follow up action on the UGC's action and on the Government circular in this context. Collect reports, information, GOI orders on education, training, employment opportunities for disabled persons and act as per policy under the programme/UGC/MHRD; and
- Work assigned from time to time to promote Higher Education for Disabled Persons under the programme."

Infrastructural Facilities in the Institutions

Whenever and wherever inclusive education system is being followed we must pay attention to their special needs. For the blind and those with low and partial vision, low vision aids, scanners and scribes (amanuenses) need to be provided. Computerized Braille print outs and talking books could be introduced for the benefit of the visually handicapped students. In the case of the hearing impaired, alternate communication strategies could be initiated. Lip reading, finger alphabets and sign language would be of great use to the hearing impaired. For those with loco-motor disabilities construction/addition of ramps/slopes, handrails and special toilets would create an environment conducive for them. In general, the disabled should be encouraged to take up technical and professional programmes rather than purely academic programmes so that they are empowered and skilled to face the future.

It is heartening to note that various Universities and colleges have taken steps to make their respective campuses architecturally accessible to the disabled. Accessibility here would refer to the "characteristic of buildings that allows for free access to a building for all purposes for which it is intended by all, including those with disabilities; often narrowly defined to focus on mobility on wheelchair-bound persons" (Building Design for Handicapped and Aged Persons 217). In order to make their campus architecturally barrier-free and disabled-friendly, ramps, slopes, hand rails and special toilets are to be constructed. At the same time, it has to be highlighted that "an environment of inclusion requires more than sympathetic campus design, staff training and technological innovation. An attitude shift involving the entire university is central to a new environment of equal access." (The ACU Bulletin 1999).

The Attitude of Teachers

The greatest obstacle which prevents the disabled from leading a normal life is the negative attitude which is prevalent in the society and even in the family of the disabled. It is this negative attitude which denies them full participation and equal opportunities.

The teachers in the educational institutions should have a positive attitude towards the disabled and develop skills to promote the disabled persons. Teachers should develop a compelling desire to be humane and academic to bring about a significant and sustainable difference in the lives of students with exceptional abilities. They should develop a vision of creating an atmosphere in which the disabled could get the maximum benefit and steps should be taken to translate to this vision into reality.

Employment of the Disabled

Adults with disabilities face major challenges in getting productive employment and independent living though they want to work and lead an independent life. It is, therefore, essential that besides general education we should also concentrate on skill training and vocational courses especially in the institutes of higher education. When they are employed they use the same community resources as the normal people and they become part of the community and contribute to its resource development by joining the work force.

Collaboration for Global Development of the Disabled

It is estimated that 80 per cent of the people with disabilities live in rural areas. People with disabilities are heterogeneous group made up of people who are born with disabilities and those who acquire a disability either due to disease or accidents. Any educational and development programme for the physically disabled should therefore involve inter-agency and Government-NGO collaboration. Even among the Government, there should be interface between various ministries so that the programmes aimed at empowering the disabled are effectively planned and implemented. Indicators to measure the disability of different type and status could be prepared and disabilities could be measured to provide appropriate care, education, and employment.

In the final analysis, development programmes rather than welfare measures should be the established target of all programmes so that the disabled are considered on par with their privileged counterparts. P.D. Mathew asserts, "A nation should be regarded as disabled if its citizens are denied equal opportunity and are excluded from mainstream activities on account of their disabilities".

33

Stress Management for Wellbeing

Stress is arousal of mind and body in response to demands made on them.

Stress is ever present, a universal feature of life. Arousal is an inevitable part of living, we constantly think, feel and act with some degree of arousal. Stress cannot and should not be avoided. Rather, it is to be maintained, managed and directed.

Stress response involves virtually every set of organs and tissues in our body. Thoughts and feelings are clearly internalised these physiological process. Body influences mind and mind influences body. The behaviour often is an outward expression of stress.

Arousal of stress is simply a part of life which everyone realises in his every day life situation. It becomes inevitable that an individual is able to manage, the, stress in his or her life.

Symptoms of Stress

The following symptoms could be observed among the people who are in stress.

Feelings

Feeling anxious, Feeling scared, Feeling irritable, Feeling moody.

Thoughts

Low self-esteem, Fear of failure, Inability to concentrate, Embarrassing easily, Worrying about the future, Preoccupation with thoughts/task, Forgetfulness.

Behaviour

Stuttering and other speech difficulties, Crying for no apparent reason, Acting impulsively, Startling easily, Laughing in a high pitch and nervous tone of voice, Grinding the teeth, Increasing use of drugs and alcohol Being accident prone, and Losing appetite or overeating.

Physiology

Perspiration/sweaty hands, Increased heart beat, Trembling Nervous ticks, Dryness of throat and mouth, Tiring easily, Urinating frequently, Sleeping problems, Diarrhea/indigestion/vomiting Butterflies in stomach, Headaches, Premenstrual tension Pain at the neck and lower back, Loss of appetite or overeating and Susceptibility to illness.

Nature of Stress

1. Stress can be positive or negative. It is a particular relationship between the person and environment that these uprights by the person as taxing or exceeding his or her resources and endangering his or her being. It focuses mainly on negative side of stress.

2. Stress is seen as a dynamic process in which the human body and mind actively respond back, engaging in continuous efforts adopt and restore balance or homeostatic.

3. Stress can be understood from a transactional process, appraisal and coping centered.

Causes of Stress: The following are some major changes in life and environment that cause stress.

Geographic mobility, Going to college, Transfer to a new school, Marriage, Pregnancy, New job, New life style, Divorce, Death of a loved one, Being fired from job, Time pressure, Competition, Financial problems, and Disappointment.

Types of Stress

There are three types of stresses. Neustress, distress and positive stress. Neustress is neutral stress arousal with neither harmful nor helpful effects one's mind or body.

Distress is too much or too little arousal, resulting in harm to mind or body.

Positive stress is helpful arousal that promotes healthy energy, satisfaction and peak performance.

Negative stress will lead to the following

Physical illness, lowered energy, decreased productivity, wasted potential to the, lack of career advancement, low self esteem, Decreased satisfaction with life, work and relationships, won involvement in public issues, joylessness and meaninglessness, absence of fun and play, absence of fun and play, open conflict, family breakups, physical abuse, high health care cost, loss of potential earnings, tension in the air, a damper on freedom of expression, and psychological put downs.

Stress related disorders

The following are some of the stress related disorders that could be observed in those who are in stress.

Migraine headaches, Tension headaches, Psoriasis, Gastritis, Ulcers, Colitis, Lower Back-pain, Chest-pain, Heart attack, Cancer, Rheumatoid arthritis, Dizzy spells, High blood-pressure, and Panic attacks.

Positive Stress helps us to

Respond quickly and forcefully in physical emergencies, helps in performing well under pressure, helps to prepare for deadlines, helps to realise potential over a period of years in athletics, academics and career. It adds zest and variety to daily life, and It helps us push our limits.

The social context of stress

Mind, body behaviour are inextricably inter-linked, stress is not only an internal quality of the person, arising entirely from forces within the person.

So each individual's experience is interwoven with the surrounding social environment- family, friends, Schools, college, workplace, temples, neighbourhood, community, region, and nation. The 'individual's experience with stress can be understood effectively and managed only by understanding the social context.

John Donne's says

"NO MAN IS AN ISLAND ENTIRE OF ITSELF'

We all face chronic pressures from the environment, the threat of nuclear war, air pollution, rising crime rates, traffic congestion, daily international tensions, the energy shortage, sexism and racism, urban noise, competition etc.

These effects are all a build-up of physical, psychological and social tensions. To overcome these stress (or) manage it, everyone should engage in seeking change in that environment when needed.

Alvin Toffler in his book Future Shock quotes that" The assertion that the world has "gone crazy" The graffiti slogan that "reality is a crutch".

Effective stress management, then includes not only self-care in pursuit of personal wellness but also includes social awareness and concern for the common good.

Dispelling common myths about stress

There are certain common myths about stress which are to be dispelled :

1. All stress is bad
2. The goal of stress management should be to eliminate stress
3. The good life should be free of stresses
4. The less the stress, the better
5. A person can always successfully adopt to difficult circumstances if he or she tries hard enough
6. Some people are destined by their heritage to be highly stressed
7. Distress has only harmful effects
8. Physical exercise drains energy that otherwise might be used to cope with stress.
9. Stress affects only adults.

Assumption about Stress Management

Whole person, life style approach to stress management is based on several guiding assumptions as :

Personal responsibility, Holism, Gradualism, Balance, Rhythm, Awareness, Action, Experiment Egoistic altruism, and Life-long process.

Stress Management for what?

- The point of stress is to enhance health and well-being for the self and for others.
- Managing stress effectively will benefit the self by improving quality of life and decreasing risk of illness.
- It will benefit those in our immediate environment by improving relationships and generating caring.
- It will benefit the wider world by directing personal energy toward improving social conditions out of which mental and physical illness, violence and other social problems arise.
- The whole point of managing stress effectively is to promote wellness for the self and for others.

The stress researches stated that:

Stress is simply the rate of response of wear and tear in the body.

In our life, actually the mind, emotion and spirit play a vital role in facing the stressful situations. In human life the individual is supposed to face the stress from the moment of conception-to-the-last breathe of the life. Stress is unavoidable part in-the human survival. Stress is a part and parcel of life. The level of stress is tolerable, then it is a thing of inspiration. Where as the level goes beyond, it will breakdown the individual personality, shatters health and becomes a danger.

How to Manage Stress?

Many stresses can be changed, eliminated or minimized. Here are a few tips that could help to manage stress:

1. They anticipate, monitor and regulate.
2. They are aware of and control their interpretations of stressors.
3. Good coppers believe they can influence events and react.
4. They practice daily deep relaxation.
5. They maintain positive health buffers-exercises, good eating habits, adequate sleep.
6. They recognise early warning signs of mental and physical distress.
7. They use constructive reactions to stress in order to reduce stress.
8. They develop and maintain a strong sense of meaning in their lives.
9. They get involved in contributing to the well-being of other persons, organisations and communities.

To conclude, it is my request that, the teachers in Higher Education Institutions are aware of the symptoms and causes of stress so that we could be efficient managers of stress and at the same time as much as possible a stress free campus could be created for the students. Today's youth are exposed to a fast changing competitive world. They are pressurised by the parents and the world around them for a new life style on completion of their education which makc them to be anxious and uncertain about their future. If proper guidance is provided to them they could cope up and manage any type of stress. It becomes the responsibility of all the Institutions of Higher Education to establish "Guidance and Counselling Centre", so that the future of India will be bright with well adjusted citizens.

Bibliography

1. Altekar, A.S. (1951), Education in Ancient India, Nand Kishore Bros, Banaras.

2. Amidon, E.J. and Elizabeth Hunter (1967). Improving Teaching the Analysis of classroom verbal instruction. Holt Rinehart and Winston, inc, Newyork.

3. Anand, Satyapal, (1979), University without halls, The Indian Perspective in Correspondence Education, Vikas Publishing House, New Delhi.

4. Blank, Thomas O., (ed.) (1992) Building Design for Handicapped and Aged Persons, McGraw Hill, New York.

5. Bloom D.S. (1956) Taxonomy of Educational objectives, cognitive Domain Book I, Moleay, New York.

6. Dourke, P. (1986), Quality measures in Universities, Common wealth Tertiary Education commission Canberra.

7. Davis, T.M., (2000) Open Doors, Report of International Exchange, The Institute of International Education New York.

8. Dayal, B. (1955) The Development of Modern Indian Education, Orient Longman, Madras.

9. Dececco, P. John (1985), The Psychology of Learning and Instruction, Prentice Hall, inc, New York.

10. Famularo Joseph (1986), Hand Book of Human Resource Planning, McGraw Hill, New York.

11. Ghosh, Suresh Chandra (1976), Educational Strategies in Developing countries, sterling publishers New Delhi.

12. Gitika Dutta Dhupkan, Vitalising the Academic Staff Colleges for improving the Quality of Teaching and Teachers in University News, Oct. 18, 1993.

13. Govt. of India, (1985) Ministry of Education, Challenge of Education, Policy Perspectives, New Delhi.

14. Govt. of India, National Policy of Education, 1986, MHRD (Dept. of Education), New Delhi.

15. Handa, S.C. Disability Provisions in India (1999) ACU Bulletin.

16. Havighurst, Robert, J. and Bernice, Society and Education, Allyn and Bacon, Boston.

17. Holmbery, Borje (1995), Theory and Practice of Distance Education, Routledge, London.

18. Jose Chander, N. (1991), Management of Distance Education sterling publishers private Ltd., New Delhi.

19. Kakkad G.M. and Seshi Gaikward, NCTE and the Universities A Diarchy (1) in Teacher Education in University News, Oct. 24, 1994.

20. Kothari D.S. Education Commission Report (1966), Government of India, Ministry of Education, New Delhi.

21. Kundu, C.L. Indian Year Book on Teacher Education (1988) Sterling Publishers Private Limited New Delhi.

22. Lockwood, F., (1998), The Design and Production of Self Instructional Materials, Kogan Page, London.

23. Mathew P D, The Rights of Persons with Disabilities (1999), Indian Social Institute, New Delhi.

24. Michael J. Dunkin (Ed.) (1987) The International Encyclopaedia of Teaching and Teacher Education Pergamon Press, New York.

25. Mohanty J. (1993) Dynamics of Higher Education in India, Deep and Deep. New Delhi.

26. Mukerjee, S.N. (1972), Education in Indra Today, Tomorrow, Acharya Book Depot, Baroda.

27. Mukhopadhyay, M. (1989) Optimising Human Learning Amar Prakashan, Delhi.

28. Nack, J.P. (1976) Equality, The Quality and Quantity–The elusive Triangle in Indian Education, Allied Publishers, Bombay.

29. NCERT Curriculum in Transaction (1978) New Delhi.

30. Pankajam, G. (2004), Reflections on Education, Gandhigram Rural University, Gandhigram 624 302.

31. Passi B.K. (1994) National Council of Teacher Education, Future Scenario and Possible Future Tasks, in University News, Nov.7.

32. Powar K.B., and S.K. Panda (1995) Higher Education in India–In search of quality, AIV Publication New Delhi.

33. Powar, K.B. (1999) Quality Assurance of Distance Education Sterling Publishers Private Ltd., New Delhi.

34. Powar, K.B. (Ed.) (1994), Environmntal Challenges and the Universitites, Association of Indian Universities, New Delhi.

35. Powar, K.B. (Ed.) (2001) Internationalisation of Indian Higher Education, Association of Indian Universities, New Delhi.

36. Powar, K.B., M.D.Tiwari and H.P. Dikshit (2002), ICT Enabled Education, AIV., New Delhi.

37. Purushothama Rao, Dr. T. and Manjula Rao, Teacher Education Programme: Am In-Depth Analysis, in Journal of All India Association for Educational Research, Sept. 1991, June 1992, Vol. 3, No. 3-4 and Vol. 4 No. 1-2.

38. Rai, A.N. (2000), Distance Education: Open Learning Vs. Virtual University concepts, author Press, New Delhi.

39. Ram Reddy, G. (ed.) (1988) Open Universities: The Ivory Towers Thrown Open, Sterling, New Delhi.

40. Sallis, E. (1993), Total Quality Management in Education Kogan page, London.

41. Seeley, Janet, Insearch of Healthy Life; Skeletal Fluorosis, Disability and Rural Livelihoods Framework, (2001), Asian Pacific Disability Rehabilitation Journal.

42. Sharma, A.P. and Usha Sharma, on professionalism among Teachers in University News, Nov. 3, 1992.

43. Sing, L.C. (1995), Multiple Models of Teaching, Vikas Publishing House, New Delhi.

44. Singh, L.C. and Sharma P.C. (1995) Teacher Education and the Teacher, Vikas Publishing House, New Delhi.

45. Skinner, B.F. (1968), The Technology of Teaching. Appletion–Century–Crofits, New York.

46. Swaran, C. Deb. (2002), Environmental Management, Jaico Publishing House, New Delhi.

47. Taher, A., and Rafik (1972) Systems Approach to Teacher Training and Curriculum Development, the case of Developing Countries, Paris: 11EP.

48. Taylor, Robert, P. (1980), Computers in the School Tuler, Tutee, Teachers' College Pocus, New York.

49. Turoff, M., (1995), Designing a Virtual Classroom, International Conference on Computer Assisted Instructions, ICCAI 1995, Hsinchu, Taiwan.

50. U.S. Educational Foundation in India (1998), Living in the USA. A Handbook for Indian Students, USEFI, New Delhi.

51. UNESCO (1998) Higher Education in the Twenty–First Century: Vision and Audios–Final Report, UNESCO, Paris.

52. University Grants Commission (1994) Accreditation and Assessment council: system and models, Operand, UGC, New Delhi.

53. World Trade Organisation (1998), Education sources, Background Note, WTO Secretariat.

Index

N

O

P